Rockhounding
Arizona

by
Gerry Blair

FALCON®
HELENA, MONTANA

© 1992 by Falcon® Publishing, Inc., Helena, Montana.
Printed in the United States of America.

6 7 8 9 0 MG 04 03 02 01 00

Falcon and FalconGuide are registered trademarks of Falcon® Publishing, Inc.

Cover photo by Eric Wunrow
Back cover photo of blood red vanadinite from Apache Mine.
All other photos by Gerry Blair

Library of Congress Cataloging-in-Publication Data
ISBN: 1-56044-389-8

CAUTION

Outdoor recreational activities are by their very nature potentially hazardous. All participants in such activities must assume the responsibility for their own actions and safety. The information contained in this guidebook cannot replace sound judgment and good decision–making skills, which help reduce risk exposure, nor does the scope of this book allow for disclosure of all the potential hazards and risks involved in such activities.

Learn as much as possible about the outdoor recreational activities you participate in, prepare for the unexpected, and be cautious. The reward will be a safer and more enjoyable experience.

♻ Text pages printed on recycled paper.

CONTENTS

ACKNOWLEDGMENTS

This part of a book, for me, is always the most difficult. Rockhounds, more than most folks, hang around with like-minded people. I am tempted to individually list every doggoned hound I have met during nearly fifty years of sniffing out rocks. I'm tempted to list every hound who has read my stuff in *Gems & Minerals*, *Lapidary Journal*, and *Rock and Gem*. You will be relieved to learn that I will not do so. I say this to those friends—thanks a heap.

In my opinion, a rockhound is not made; a rockhound grows. And the way I see it, his or her communion with others in the hobby allows and encourages that growth. Knowing that, I wish to specifically thank the following hounds. I owe a special debt to O.B. "Bud" Marshall of Granada Hills, California. Bud generously shared detailed maps of mineral and gemstone locations. Martin Koning of Morristown, Arizona, (Koning Lapidaries) shared information on other locations. Thanks, Martin and Bud. Much that is good in this book can be credited to your generosity.

I owe special thanks to W.R.C. Shedenhelm, Senior Editor of *Rock and Gem Magazine* (although he will be semi-retired at time of publication). Bill Shedenhelm encouraged my rock writing over the years and has been a constant friend (even though we met only once, and then, only briefly).

Thanks also to the late Lou Boettcher, who was a pleasant companion during rock collecting trips to the Rowley, Red Cloud, Four Peaks, and too many more to mention. Wherever you happen to be, Lou old buddy, you are not forgotten. Doug McVicar of Kingman, Arizona, is another good-un. Doug and I have cooperated on lapidary and silver-working projects. Doug and Lorraine are the best of rockhound friends.

Finally, heartfelt thanks to Larry Gates of Congress, Arizona, who has shared more than a few hunts with me, and to Mark Middleton of Four Seasons Color Labs, who took special effort to ensure that the photos used in this book were processed as well as could be.

MAP LEGEND

Interstate		Interstate	$\boxed{00}$
Paved Road		U. S. Highway	(00)
Improved Dirt Road		State Highway	[00]
Primitive Road		Principal Road	(375)
Bridge		Forest Road	0000
Gate		Reservation Road	00
Cattle Guard		Campground	▲
Foot Trail		Pass or Saddle	
Railroad		Mountain(s)	
Gem Material Location		Hills	
Mine	⊙	Rim	
Pit		River	
Building	■	Creek	
Shaft		Dry Wash	
National and State Parks		Lakes	
Gem Site Location in Arizona		Meadow or Swamp	
		Springs	
		Petrified Wood	

SITE LOCATIONS

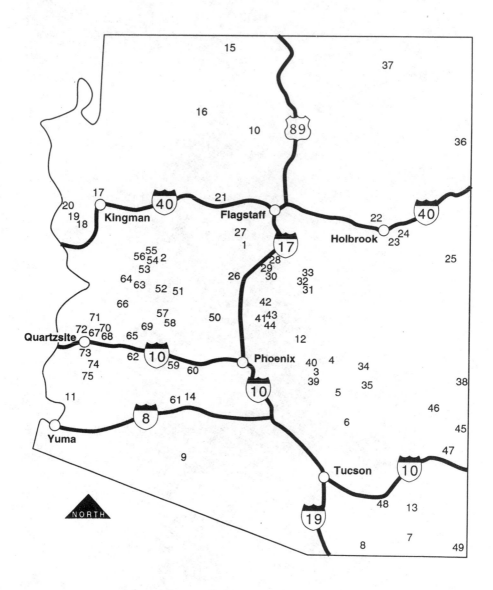

Gads and hammers can help liberate rock and minerals.

ABOUT THIS BOOK

Some rockhound guidebooks consist of a series of maps and terse instructions directing the reader to a string of sites where rocks and minerals have been found. Too often, those areas were picked clean years ago. Sometimes the collecting area listed is no longer accessible. Some have been posted against trespassing. Others have been incorporated into wilderness areas and are now off limits to motor vehicles.

This is not that kind of book. The author and the publisher are convinced that rockhounds and mineral hounds have an intense interest in information other than where to collect. We believe they have an interest in every aspect of the rock and mineral hobby—collecting minerals, preparing gems, and displaying their finds. But rockhounds are also drawn to the landscape, to the sites and artifacts of prehistoric peoples, and to natural phenomena, such as northern Arizona's meteor crater. This mile-wide pock on Earth's crust—the largest impact crater in North America—was formed 50,000 years ago when a meteoric mass that weighed as much as twenty million tons struck the earth at supersonic speed. Precisely the sort of anecdote to pique a rockhound's interest. Rock and mineral collectors have an interest in Petrified Forest National Park and the fossils there. Rockhounds, as we see it, have an interest in mines and mining history, in plants and animals they are likely to encounter as they pursue the hobby, and in public exhibits of rocks, minerals, fossils, and other curiosities.

Rockhounding Arizona, therefore, makes an honest effort to guide the reader to all that is of geological interest within the state. If a listed area is depleted or nearly so, that will be mentioned. Or if rocks or minerals could be recovered only after back-breaking work, that will be mentioned. You will not be able to collect at some of the areas mentioned. For example, the garnet and peridot locales on tribal reservations that we list are now closed to collecting by non-tribal members. Some older guidebooks list the areas as accessible. We've tried to provide up-to-date information as a service to the reader, which may prevent an unfortunate confrontation. However, specific directions to these closed areas are included so that the collector will have the necessary information in the event collecting regulations change, as they sometimes do.

Nearly all of the mines listed are closed to underground collecting. Nearly all are shored with dry-rotted timbers, deteriorated ladders, and fractured ground. Some have bad air. Others are a haven for creepy crawlies of the most disgusting kind. Most of these properties will yield up specimen rock to the collector who is willing to work the dump. Why mention the mines at all? For a number of good reasons. Most have played a part in the history of Arizona. Many have contributed fine mineral specimens, at times the best in the world, to prestigious museums.

The listing of a rock or mineral location does not guarantee access. Areas known to be closed to collecting will be identified, and areas known to be

Copper, Arizona's state mineral, is found in superb crystallizations.

open to collecting will be identified. Even so, the status can change overnight. Each reader has a responsibility to verify the status before he or she enters the area to collect.

Specific directions are provided for most collecting sites. A few of the areas are less specifically described. The reason for this is because no specific information is available (as with The Mystery Plume of the Peloncillos) or because the deposit itself is non-specific, covering an extended area (as with Patriotic Agate north of Brenda). Some of the collecting sites can be dangerous. Mines are the most obvious example. More subtle dangers exist at other sites. Some are located at the end of a long hike made at high elevation (Amethyst at Four Peaks and others). Only the most physically fit will be able to visit the site.

Other collecting sites, even though above ground, have treacherous ground (Amethyst at Four Peaks is again cited). Cave-ins have killed collectors who ignored private property rights and who disregarded hazard warnings. Finally, the Arizona wild country can be cruel to those who do not have the correct equipment or who tackle the backcountry with the wrong attitude. A trip to a collecting site in the desert can be fun-filled during the winter months. That same trip can be a nightmare during the summer, a time when daytime temperatures will exceed 100 degrees every doggoned day until winter comes. It is not our intent to discourage, nor to frighten collectors away from a hobby that is inherently safe. We feel obligated to point out potential problems. Common sense precautions, nearly always, prevent trouble.

INTRODUCTION TO ARIZONA

Arizona has been called the Baby State because it was the last of the contiguous forty-eight admitted to the Union. It is a pretty big baby, ranking sixth in size among the lower forty-eight. The name Arizona comes from Arizonac, an early name for the territory, and Arizonac comes from the Tohono O'odham words *ali*, meaning small, and *shonak*, meaning place of the spring. The territory was awarded statehood on February 14, 1912. The desert legume called the palo verde (Spanish for green stick) is the state tree. This inconspicuous desert dweller turns splendent during April as the green-barked limbs explode with a riot of yellow blossoms. Another desert dweller, the saguaro cactus, produces the state flower during late spring. The showy white blossoms bud and bloom from the arm tips of this ponderous cactus during the second half of May. The state bird is the cactus wren, a perky bird that sometimes nests in the palo verde and sometimes eats the bugs that hang around the waxy blossoms of the saguaro.

Copper is the state mineral—not surprising when you consider that the half-handful of major and minor copper producers in the state have produced more than 500 billion pounds of the red metal. Arizona is ranked the number one copper producer in the United States. Those prolific tunnels, shafts, and pits in Arizona have produced more than copper: more minerals, in fact, than can be mentioned. There's lapidary rough such as azurite, malachite, chrysocolla, and others. And turquoise. Tons of the good stuff, which, naturally, is Arizona's state gemstone. The best of the best from the Morenci Pit (Clifton), the Lavender Pit (Bisbee), the Sleeping Beauty (Miami), and Ithaca Peak (Kingman) has been declared the best in the world.

THE LANDSCAPE

Arizona's 113,909-square-mile surface is a land of radical contrasts. Elevation varies from 12,670 feet atop Mount Humphrey in the San Francisco Peaks to 137 feet above sea level at Yuma. Annual precipitation varies with elevation and latitude. The summer-home area at Crown King, within the Bradshaw Mountain Range, averages 32.42 inches of precipitation, while Yuma, down in the lowlands, receives a miserly 3.1 inches. Even though Arizona is large, population density is moderate. About three million friendly folks (and a few old grumps) call the copper state home. Most of that three million live in the population centers of greater Phoenix and greater Tucson.

Arizona can be divided into three general land types. The northern third of the state, an area sometimes called the Colorado Plateau, the Arizona Plateau, or the Coconino Plateau, has a mean elevation of 6,500 feet. Here, volcanic summits reach to 10,000 feet and higher. Although part of this land mass is plateau-like, much consists of grand canyons (yep, the Grand Canyon is one such), gorges, coulees, and gullies. Much of the area is forested by the largest unbroken ponderosa pine stand in the world. Annual snowfall can be impressive. During the winter of 1991-1992, more than ten feet of snow fell on Flagstaff. The Snow Bowl ski area within the San Francisco Peaks sometimes receives twice that. Wildlife abounds in this plateau country. Rocky Mountain elk (wapiti), pronghorn, bison, and two species of deer are the primary herbivores. Wild turkeys and band-tailed pigeons roost among the ponderosa. The predator list is impressive, including black bear, mountain lion, bobcat, coyote, two species of fox, raccoons, ringtail cats (cacomistles), and coati mundi. The handsome Abert's and Kaibab squirrels, both boasting tufted ears, show a blue-gray coat and a snow-white tail.

The second geographic division is the Basin Range, about 68,000 square miles of land that begins below the impressive escarpment called the Mogollon (say muggy-on) Rim. Some call this jumble of mountains, hills, and forest the transition woodlands. Oak and several kinds of juniper prevail.

The third general geographic division is the plains, an area that includes true plains and desert. Much of the land is flat, or nearly so, interspersed with substantial mountain ranges. Much of the area called the plains is arid low country—desert. It is a country filled with odd life forms, such as the multi-ton mega-cactus called the saguaro, and the cholla that is sometimes called the jumping cactus (no, it can't jump). The thorny balls are so precariously attached to the stem that the lightest touch causes them to detach, sometimes into the tender body of a rockhound. Smart collectors here carry a pair of tweezers, just in case. And there are monsters. Really. A foot-and-a-half long rainbow-colored lizard named the gila monster. Can the gila monster bite? Yes. Is the bite poisonous? Yes, again. The good news? Don't mess with the monster and the monster likely will not mess with you. Actually, consider yourself fortunate if you even glimpse one of these shy and rare reptiles. If you do see one, know that the monster is a protected species here in Arizona. Many areas of rockhound interest lie within the plains, particularly within the desert. And nearly all of the plains area is on public land accessible to the rock and mineral collector.

Only about fifteen percent of Arizona is privately owned. Much of the remainder is public land managed by the State Land Department, the Bureau of Land Management (BLM), or the United States Department of Agriculture Forest Service (USFS). Some of the public lands are closed to collecting, including military bases, tribal reservations, and national parks and monuments. Other lands, such as wilderness areas closed to motor vehicles, pose significant difficulties for mineral collectors. Even though collecting may be legal in such places, the average rockhound cannot or will not walk dozens of mile to gather a load of rock. What is left after the restricted areas are deducted? A hell of a lot of land, and maybe more—plenty of land to roam, containing agates and jaspers in mind-boggling variety, and more than 640 mineral species.

The rockhound menu for Arizona is impressive: agate and jaspers of infinite variety, some of the best facet-grade amethyst in the world (Four Peaks), some of the best facet-grade pyrope garnet in the world (Four Corners area), some of the best facet-grade peridot in the world (Peridot and Four

Corners), a colossal collection of petrified wood—petrified rainbows encased in solid chalcedony and jasper (Petrified Forest National Park and surrounding lands), turquoise, chrysocolla silicate, wulfenite, azurite, copper, and too many others to mention. For many rockhounds, that is as good as it gets.

THE BOLA TIE

Even though most states have state flowers, state birds, and even state rocks, Arizona is the only state that can claim a state neckwear. The 1971 Arizona Legislature signed into law a statute making the bola tie the official neckwear of Arizona.

This stylized peyote bird carries a load of Bisbee turquoise.

WHATnHEK IS a bola tie? It is a cord of braided leather decorated with a bola—from Spanish for ball—made from gemstone, jewelry, or other material. A scorpion carcass embalmed in acrylic is one example; a more palatable tie might feature turquoise or petrified wood. The cord tips are almost always likewise decorated, mostly with formed silver cones called bola tips. Wickenburg resident Vic Cedarstaff is generally credited as the developer of the bola tie in 1949. The 1971 statute recognizes Cedarstaff as the namer and originator of the novel neckwear. Photographs dating to the 1920s, however, show that the "string tie" was available and in use then. Nearly everyone agrees, though, that Vic Cedarstaff gave the bola tie its name and developed a technique for manufacturing the yoke slide that holds the decoration to the leather cord. What is the penalty for not wearing a bola instead of a four-in hand or a power tie? The worst imaginable. The home folk will assume you are a snowbird, or worse, a dude. Some might be discourteous enough to say so right out loud. Think of it this way: as a rockhound, wearing a bola tie affords you the opportunity to exhibit a part of your gemstone collection.

SIGHTS TO SEE

Mining is important to Arizona. The proliferation of large and small mines within the state has contributed billions of dollars to the state's economy, though most of those mines are inactive now. The New Cornelia Pit at Ajo no longer thunders to the roar of massive machinery. The Lavender Pit at Bisbee, and the tunnels, stopes, and rooms that feed from the Cole Shaft are equally quiet. The Duval property north of Kingman (Ithaca Peak) has shut down.

Only three major mines continue limited production: the Miami Inspiration Copper Company at Miami, the Phelps Dodge pit at Morenci, and the Cyprus property at Bagdad.

During the days of production, Arizona mines contributed more than metal. Spectacular crystallizations and ore samples of more than 640 separate mineral species have been identified within Arizona ores. Some crystals and ores are on public display at museums across the state.

The Arizona State Mining and Mineral Museum is a fine place for a rockhound to spend a day. Much of that time should be spent viewing the mineral specimens contained within the Woolery Collection. Other exhibits feature amethyst from Four Peaks, a six-foot hunk of native copper, a 113-pound quartz crystal, and a 250-pound piece of azurite/malachite from the Copper Queen Mine at Bisbee. Also noteworthy are displays of lapidary, fluorescents, fossils, and meteorites. The Mining and Mineral Museum has moved from the fairgrounds and is now quartered at 1502 W. Washington, Phoenix, AZ 85007. Museum hours are 8 a.m. to 5 p.m. Monday through Friday. Saturday hours are 1 p.m. to 5 p.m. The museum is closed on Sundays and legal holidays. Admission is free.

Near Tucson, the Arizona-Sonora Desert Museum offers an excellent earth science and mineral display. The museum and accompanying zoo are housed in Tucson Mountain Park a few miles west of Tucson. An outstanding collection of gems and minerals are on display. A large walk-through, man-made cave and mine offers a look at pockets of minerals reconstructed to simulate their natural occurrence. The zoo displays many of the animals of the Sonoran Desert in spacious enclosures that simulate natural habitat. The mountain lion and desert bighorn sheep enclosures are particularly fine. The museum is open daily from 8:30 a.m. to 5 p.m. from September 16 through March 14, and daily from 7:30 a.m. to 6 p.m. the remainder of the year. An admission fee is charged. Contact Arizona-Sonora Desert Museum, 2021 N. Kinney Road, Tucson, AZ 85743.

In Tucson, the Department of Geosciences at the University of Arizona maintains a mineral museum. The collection is complete, displaying outstanding minerals, crystals, rocks, ores, and fossils. The nearby Arizona State Museum provides a look at the past with its historical exhibits.

The Arizona Historical Society Museum, across the street from the University, features a walk-through exhibit displaying a reconstructed mine and a stamp mill. Part of the exhibit features mineral specimens.

Also in Tuscon, the Old Pueblo Museum is small, but it offers a quality collection of Arizona gems and minerals. Look for it as part of the Foothills Mall.

Perhaps the finest meteorite display in the U.S. is found within the collection of Arizona State University at Tempe. Other gem and mineral exhibits can be seen at Northern Arizona University, Flagstaff; the Museum of Northern Arizona, Flagstaff; Meteor Crater, east of Flagstaff; Petrified Forest National Park, east of Holbrook; and the small but interesting collection maintained by Jim Gray at the Crystal Forest Museum at the south gate of Petrified Forest National Park.

PETRIFIED FOREST NATIONAL PARK

The petrified logs here boggle the mind. Two hundred feet long and half a man high, the multi-ton monsters are a rainbow of petrified color. The wood fibers have been replaced with a colorful chalcedony. The somewhat mysterious process of petrification began nearly 200 million years ago as the living trees fell and sank into swampy lowlands. Protected from parasites by a mile-thick blanket of earth and water, silica-rich water percolated through the wood cells. Millions of years later, erosion and other phenomena caused the huge fossils to emerge.

Ample evidence shows that aboriginal humans existed within the area that is now the petrified forest, dating from about the time of the birth of Christ. The first modern people to visit the area were likely the Spanish. A 1549 document contains a reference to *desierto pintado*—the painted desert, a nearby feature. As civilization moved westward, exploitation of the forest logs occurred. President Theodore Roosevelt, using the power granted by the Act For the Preservation of American Antiquities (passed June 8, 1906), named the area a national monument on December 8, 1906. Full national park status was awarded in 1962.

Many of the 750,000 annual visitors to the park allow themselves a hurried tour. They exit Interstate 40 to make a quick two-hour drive along the forest highway. They see the logs and maybe even take time to see and photograph the Rio Puerco Ruins. Then it is back to the interstate to head west to Disneyland or east toward home. Rockhounds almost always want more. Their special knowledge allows a fuller understanding of the magnificence of the petrification process. The logs are the most prominent feature within the park and are the largest fossils found here. Other fossils are also abundant. The visitor centers offer a look at ferns and other plant fossils. Ossified bones of ancient reptiles are on display. Part of the visitor center documents prehistoric people's residence in the area.

Rockhounds who have the time and energy necessary to hike the park (a permit is needed) have a further opportunity. They can enjoy a close-up look at petroglyphs and pictographs. It is likely they will encounter metates and manos, bowls and handstones used to grind beans, grains, and corn. Persistent hikers might discover The Cave of Life, located near Newspaper Rock. Petroglyphs within the cave show stick figures in the act of copulation.

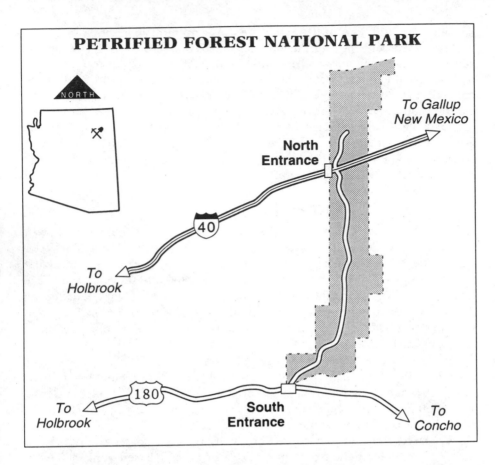

PETRIFIED FOREST NATIONAL PARK

North Entrance

To Gallup New Mexico

To Holbrook

To Holbrook

South Entrance

To Concho

Park personnel speculate that young folks from the Rio Puerco Ruins came here to escape summer boredom and to do the things many young folks have done since time began. Rock writing of a different kind can be found in a cave east of the Rio Puerco Ruins. Aboriginal artists used a paint made of powdered limonite, blood, and urine to decorate the low roof of a cave.

Petrified Forest National Park can accurately be called a rockhound's park. Nearly every feature corresponds to an important interest within the hobbyist's realm. And even though **collecting is prohibited** for obvious reasons (rangers watch visitors through binoculars and sometimes conduct car searches), any rockhound worth the name will consider his or her time spent here a wise allotment. Smart visitors bring their cameras and avail themselves of the numerous photographic opportunities. The images of park attractions can keep the joy of the visit fresh for a lifetime.

GRAND CANYON NATIONAL PARK

The great gash that contains the Colorado River is the grandest canyon of them all. This immense geologic feature, taken into the national park system in 1916, has been photographed by a camera-carrying satellite from 570 miles up. Even at that altitude, the Grand Canyon remains GRAND.

The red and rose rocks of the canyon present a pleasing aspect to nearly all eyes. The eyes of the rock and mineral hound will register an extra measure of pleasure, though **no mineral, fossil, or artifact collecting is allowed within the National Park**. The mile-high walls of the Grand Canyon display millions of years of geology. Fossils are obvious in much of the rock. Mines within the Grand Canyon have yielded up rare minerals and crystals, at times the best examples of a particular kind found anywhere in the world.

Garcia Lopez de Cardenas, a member of the Coronado Expedition, was the first European to view the canyon, in 1540. Other explorations followed. Major John Wesley Powell, during his second float of the Big Canyon, as it was then called, changed its name to Grand Canyon.

The canyon varies from a depth of 3,000 feet to 6,000 feet. Width varies from four to fifteen miles. One hundred and five miles of the Grand Canyon are protected in Grand Canyon National Park. Many well-maintained trails provide access to those hardy hikers who hanker to see the canyon from the bottom up.

The most often asked question at the Grand Canyon is, "What happened here?" There is no simple answer to such a complex question. The bright ribbon of water at the canyon bottom, some say, is responsible for what happened. Others claim that wind and water cooperated to erode the canyon walls, grain by grain. Another school of thought maintains that volcanism and uplifting are responsible. Actually, the canyon was likely formed by a combination of all those forces.

Fossils of varying age are obvious within much of the exposed rock. The Toroweap and the Kaibab (Permian) offer a look at fish, crustaceans, brachiopods, bryozoans, corals, crinoids, and others. Cambrian sea fossils (Paleozoic) include fine specimens of the trilobite *D. Olenellus*. Devonian and Mississippian coral are well represented. The Pennsylvanian and the Early Permian yield up plant remains and animal trackways.

A fossil of recent times was found in one of the caves that pock the wall of the north rim. Rampart Cave, containing a 160-foot arm, was a hangout for a giant, 400-pound sloth. The beast left a cave full of well-preserved poop. Scattered within the dung were skeletons of the sloth. Willis Evans, a Native American, discovered the cave during the hot summer of 1936. Even though the remote location offered protection and the cave was within the Grand Canyon National Park, an intruder's torch later caused the dry dung to ignite. The fire was discovered in July 1976. The National Park Service struggled for many months to contain the fire. When it was extinguished, examination showed that much of the archaeological value had been destroyed.

Grand Canyon mining activity peaked between 1860 and 1900. Nearly every side canyon was investigated. Some claims were filed, and a great deal of exploratory work was done. Some of the properties even shipped ore. Few, however, turned a profit. The mines offered hard work for small reward. The remote aspect and the rough terrain caused significant shipping costs.

Two mines, The Grandview Copper and the Mooney Lead Mine in Carbonate Canyon, have been discussed elsewhere in this book. Other mines near the Carbonate Canyon property gave up silver, vanadium, galena, and sphalerite. One property within these Bridal Veil Mines (the falls are now called Havasupai Falls) was located 250 feet up a sheer cliff. An iron scaffolding was constructed to support a wood ladder that lead to the tunnel entrance. Extraordinary crystals of vanadinite coating calcite were found.

Other somewhat important Grand Canyon mines were the Grand Gulch (Grand Wash Cliffs, copper) and the Orphan Mine. The Grand Gulch was located in 1853. Samuel Adams, one of the locators, is said to have bought the rights to the mine for a horse and a few pounds of flour.

The Orphan, located on the south rim of the canyon, was located as a copper property. Daniel Hogan, an orphan, filed his claim in 1893, calling it the Lost Orphan Mine. The mine offered lots of hard work but little profit and became inactive. It was offered new life in 1951 when the Geological Survey discovered ore rich in uranium. The Orphan is the only mine currently operating within Grand Canyon National Park.

River runners will notice a series of large steel towers on the north side of the canyon 266 miles downriver from Lees Ferry. The towers, 800 feet above the river, supported cables that transported bat guano from caves within the north rim to the south rim.

President Theodore Roosevelt declared the area around the canyon a Game Reserve during 1906 in an attempt to protect the world-famous deer herd that summered here. The deer eventually reproduced beyond the land's capacity to support them, and a massive die-off took place. Two years later,

Many large meteorite fragments have been found on public land surrounding the impact site of Arizona's Meteor Crater.

Roosevelt upgraded protection and the Grand Canyon National Monument was formed. President Woodrow Wilson signed enabling legislation in 1919 to award full national park status.

METEOR CRATER

The huge meteoric mass was traveling at an estimated 45,000 miles per hour when it approached Earth's atmosphere. Heat produced by friction caused the mass to begin breaking up as it entered the atmosphere. Even so, impact caused a cone-shaped hole 570 feet deep, one mile across, and more than three miles in circumference. The crater, nearly 50,000 years after impact, remains the best preserved meteorite impact site on Earth.

Meteor Crater is an awe-inspiring sight. Privately owned, the area has been developed to allow visitor enjoyment. Observation platforms allow safe viewing. A well-stocked gift shop offers a multitude of interesting items, including some lapidary items.

What happened to the meteorite? The breakup, caused by friction and the resultant heat created by the Earth's atmosphere, was accelerated on impact. Much of the material likely exploded back into the air to fall as solidified fragments of nickel-iron. The largest piece recovered is a hefty 1,406-pound piece, on display at the crater.

No collecting is allowed within the area of the crater. Specimens from the crater are for sale at the gift shop. The force of the impact caused

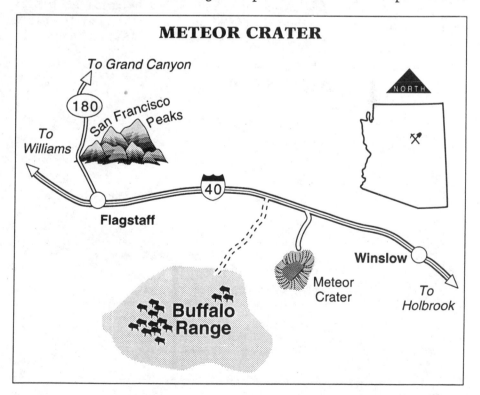

meteorite fragments (each actually a miniature meteorite) to rain over a considerable distance surrounding the crater. Collectors with sharp eyes have been able to collect specimens from those public lands. A specimen in the author's collection is the size of a hen's egg (extra large) and has the typical pocked exterior. The interior is bright nickel-iron.

A metal detector might assist the search for meteor fragments. The soil, however, contains a lot of iron dust that could cause the detector to become confused. Meteor Crater is located a few miles south of Interstate 40 between the towns of Flagstaff and Winslow. The access road is blacktopped, as is the parking lot.

THE LOST DUTCHMAN

Gold-hungry hunters have marched through the rattlesnake-infested hotlands of central Arizona for more than 100 years. Each had a similar goal: to find the fabled Lost Dutchman gold mine or to find a gold mine with similar riches.

Jacob Walz called himself a Deutschman. Contemporaries called him "The Dutchman." He was a German immigrant who came to Arizona during the 1860s and homesteaded 160 acres of desert in an area now within central Phoenix.

The Dutchman and his burros spent much of their time prospecting the sere Superstition Mountain Range that loomed fifty miles east. Occasionally he would visit surrounding towns to trade a gold-laced quartz for supplies. He eventually abandoned the hard life of the prospector and retired to a modest home in Phoenix. He died there on October 25, 1881 (of pneumonia

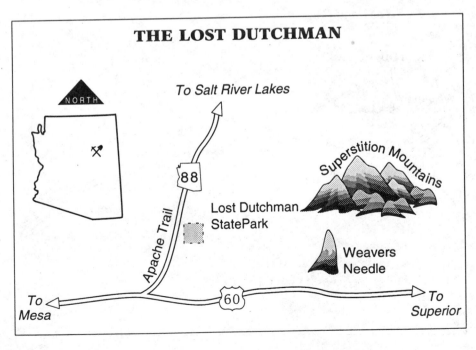

contracted as he clung to a tree for three days during a flood). He was buried in a cemetery southeast of the state capitol. There is no headstone.

Some say Jacob Walz had no mine; that he discovered a cached treasure belonging to the Jesuits. Others, noting the similarity between The Dutchman's gold and gold produced from the Vulture Mine (near Wickenburg), speculate that Walz bought stolen gold from Vulture miners and concocted the rich mine story to cover the source. Still others, a hell of a lot of others, are convinced that the mine did and does exist.

Former Arizona Attorney General Bob Corbin is one of the latter. Corbin, a persistent Lost Dutchman Mine hunter, claims he has held samples of the Dutchman's ore in his hand. An assay conducted in the 1890s showed that the ore was worth more than $100,000 to the ton. And that was computed when gold was worth a bit more than $20 per ounce. That same ore, at today's gold price, would assay a mind-boggling one million dollars a ton. Modern testing by the University of Arizona School of Mines, Corbin says, shows that the ore came from no known mine within the state.

Does the Lost Dutchman Mine exist? Will it someday be found? No one knows. Even so, herds of prospectors continue to hunt the Superstitions, not deterred by the shootings and the deaths that have been a part of the search. For them, the end of the rainbow rests somewhere within the Superstitions. The pot of gold that might be found there keeps them searching.

ARIZONA TRIBAL LANDS

Fifteen Indian reservations transect the Arizona landscape. These lands, set aside for the exclusive use of the various Native American tribes, range in size from the sprawling Navajo Reservation, with fourteen million acres and 200,000 residents, to the diminutive Payson Apache Reservation, with eighty-five acres and a few dozen occupants. Each reservation governs its lands by an elected body called a tribal council. Each reservation determines rules and regulations that control the behavior of non-tribal visitors; thus, **rock and mineral collecting regulations will vary from reservation to reservation**.

NAVAJO

The Navajo (NA-vah-ho) call themselves *Dine*—the people. Their 22,610-square-mile reservation is located mainly in Arizona but extends into the neighboring states of Utah and New Mexico. The Navajo Reservation is the largest such reservation in the world, larger than Connecticut, Massachusetts, Rhode Island, and New Jersey combined. The land within the reservation varies from grazed rangelands near Tuba City to lush alpine forests and meadowlands, north of Window Rock. Many Navajo occupy remote dwellings called hogans and make a living raising cattle, sheep, and goats.

meadowlands, north of Window Rock. Many Navajo occupy remote dwellings called hogans and make a living raising cattle, sheep, and goats.

A number of gem and gemstone deposits are located on Navajo lands. The garnet (Garnet Ridge) and peridot (Buell Park) deposits are described elsewhere in this book. Two interesting deposits of colorful petrified wood deserve mention here. The first is located near Nazlini, south of Canyon de Chelly (say shay). The wood here is well preserved and is the same sort of rainbow wood that can be found within Petrified Forest National Park and surrounding lands. Like the Petrified Forest, the Chinle formation that holds the wood on the Navajo Reservation is a greasy clay that turns slick when wet. A second wood deposit lies near the small village of Sanoste in the foothills of the Chuska Mountains, on the New Mexico part of the reservation. The Sanoste wood shows excellent bark preservation. While the interior is an uninteresting mottle of dull grays, the crust is colored an excellent green. The Sanoste wood is a marginal lapidary material but is an excellent specimen material.

A number of tufa deposits dot this vast reservation, the best quality found at the deposit near Red Lake, northeast of Tuba City. Tufa is a fine-grained volcanic tuff that can be used as a mold in jewelry making. The best material can be carved with a pocket knife. Molten metal (usually silver) poured into the carved void hardens to form attractive casts, often reproducing the texture of the tufa to deliver a pebbled surface. Many Navajo silversmiths use the tufa to produce attractive bolas, bracelets, ketohs (bow guards), and pendants.

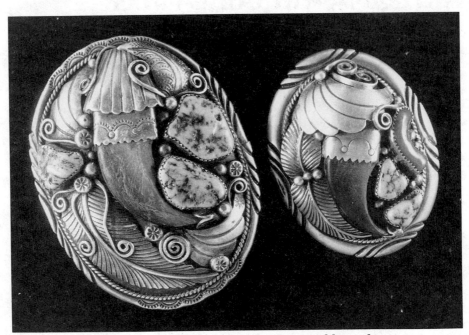

Navajo jewelry often incorporates turquoise, silver, and bear claws.

made by Navajo women, are available at arts and crafts shops located near reservation population centers.

For current information, contact the Navajo Nation, Window Rock, AZ 86515; phone (602) 871-4941).

SAN CARLOS APACHE

The San Carlos Apache Reservation bounds slightly less than two million acres. Although a small part of the reservation is covered by ponderosa pine (Big Prairie above The Nantac Rim), most reservation land is high desert. The main industry here is cattle ranching. Tourism, in recent years, has become a close competitor.

The peridot deposit at Peridot Mesa and the andradite garnet deposit at Stanley Butte will be discussed in detail elsewhere in this book. The tribe also operates an enterprise called Tsee Yo' Ba Gowa (stone bead house) that offers faceted and tumbled peridot.

A deposit of the colorful chalcedony called fire agate is located near the southeastern border of the San Carlos Apache Reservation. The Slaughter Mountain (named for Pete Slaughter, an early cattleman) chalcedony yields up some of the finest fire agate found. Many of the pieces combine a complement of reds, greens, blues, and oranges to produce a gem of unusual beauty. **As with other gemstone deposits on the San Carlos Apache lands, the Slaughter Mountain fire agate deposit is closed to non-tribal collecting. The entire area, at present, is closed to non-tribal entry.** Some San Carlos Apache occasionally collect here, however, and fire agate rough is sometimes available. Matthew Hopkins Sr., a ranger for the San Carlos Recreation and Wildlife Department, can usually supply information on the availability of fire agate and rough peridot. Contact him at P.O. Box 593, Peridot, AZ 85542. Information about recreational opportunities on the San Carlos Indian Reservation can be obtained from The San Carlos Recreation and Wildlife Department, P.O. Box 97, San Carlos, AZ 85550; phone (602) 475-2343.

TOHONO O'ODHAM (PAPAGO)

The Papago Indian Reservation, now called the Tohono O'odham by tribal decree, occupies nearly three million acres and has a population of about 10,000. The southern boundary of the reservation is also the boundary between the United States and Mexico. A strong Mexican influence can be noticed in language and custom. The main industry here is cattle ranching. The main arts and crafts products are baskets woven of native materials. Tohono O'odham baskets show a diverse form, many emulating anthropomorphic (human-like) and zoomorphic (animal-like) shapes. An arts and crafts cooperative at Sells, and trading posts here, offer a fine selection. The Tohono O'odham manufacture about 5,000 baskets yearly, more than any other Native American tribe.

The reservation holds a number of geologically interesting sites. A fortification agate containing alternating bands of gray and white has been found near Chuichu (Pima for caves). Copper mines in the Vekol (Pima for grandmother) Mountains have yielded interesting specimen material. Abandoned manganese mines at various locations have provided excellent specimens of manganite. For information about current recreational regulations, contact The Tohono O'odham Tribe, P.O. Box 837, Sells, AZ 85634; phone (602) 383-2221.

Other Arizona reservations offer gem, gemstone, and mineral specimens. A list of tribal addresses, and a map showing approximate locations of each, follows.

Ak-Chin Indian Community
Route 1, Box 12
Maricopa, AZ 85239
(602) 568-2227

Cocopah Tribal Council
P.O. Bin "G"
Somerton, AZ 85350
(602) 627-2102

Colorado River Indian Tribes
Route-1, Box 23-B
Parker, AZ 85344
(602) 669-9211

Fort McDowell Mohave-Apache
Community Council
P.O. Box 17779
Fountain Hills, AZ 85258
(602) 990-0995

Fort Mohave Indian Tribe
500 Marriman
Needles, CA 92363
(619) 326-4591

Gila River Indian Community
P.O. Box 97
Sacaton, AZ 85247
(602) 562-3311

Havasupai Tribal Council
General Delivery
Supai, AZ 86435
(602) 448-2961

Hopi Tribe
P.O. Box 123
Oraibi, AZ 86039
(602) 734-2441

Hualapai Tribal Council
P.O. Box 168
Peach Springs, AZ 86434
(602) 769-2216

Kaibab Band of Paiute Indians
P.O. Box 302
Fredonia, AZ 86022
(602) 643-7245

Navajo Nation
Window Rock, AZ 86515
(602) 871-4941

The Tohono O'odham Tribe
of Arizona
P.O. Box 837
Sells, AZ 85634
(602) 383-2221

Pascua Yaqui Tribal Council
4821 West Calle Vicam
Tucson, AZ 85706
(602) 883-2838

Payson Indian Community
Council
(Yavapai-Tonto Apache Tribe)
Box 184
Payson, AZ 85541
(602) 474-5000

ARIZONA

TRIBAL LANDS

Quechan Tribal Council
(Fort Yuma Indian Reservation)
P.O. Box 11352
Yuma, AZ 85364
(619) 572-0213

Salt River-Pima Maricopa
Tribal Council
Route 1, Box 216
Scottsdale, AZ 85256
(602) 941-7277

San Carlos Apache Tribe
P.O. Box O
San Carlos, AZ 85550
(602) 475-2361

White Mountain Apache Tribe
(Fort Apache Indian Reservation)
P.O. Box 700
Whiteriver, AZ 85941
(602) 338-4346

Yavapai-Apache Community Council
Camp Verde Indian Reservation
Clarkdale, AZ 86324
(602) 567-3649

Yavapai-Prescott
Community Association
530 E. Merritt St.
Prescott, AZ 86301
(602) 445-8790

ARIZONA WILDLIFE

Many rockhounds who visit the wild and wooly westlands for the first time do not realize they must share the turf with an amazing variety of resident wildlife. Usually the critters are content to live and let live. Most will steal silently away at the first footfall or the faraway purr of a pickup motor. Infrequently, human/critter confrontations occur. The well-prepared collector should be able to identify a few of the critters. The following paragraphs will help you identify them—and separate the "bad guys" from the "good guys."

The javelina (pronounced have-ah-LEAN-ah) is more properly called a collared peccary. This pig-like animal weighs fifty pounds, tops, although he may look much bigger when he has his hair at attention, tusks clacking. Javelina normally run in packs called sounders. The pigs make their living by ripping apart cactus and other desert growth with their tusks. They are not hostile toward rockhounds. They can be hostile, however, toward a rockhound's hound, particularly when the pooch decides to impress the boss by running that herd of hairy pigs out of the county. Unless the pooch is a Russian wolfhound who has a black belt in Karate, chances are good he will be enthusiastically dissected.

You will almost certainly hear—and sometimes sight—the wild desert dog, the coyote, while on an Arizona rockhound trip. Like the javelina, the coyote is an animal that prefers to keep its own company. Almost any coyote, it

The western collared lizard is not poisonous but can inflict a painful bite.

18

should be noted, will evidence an intense interest in a rockhound's pet. That interest can be intensified if the coyote is hungry and if the pet is bite-sized or close to bite-sized. Many a rockhound poodle has left camp to go wee-wee and has never returned.

A healthy coyote will seldom stay in sight long. Experience has taught coyotes that humans carry bang-sticks that can inflict pain at an amazing distance. Unhealthy coyotes, particularly rabid ones, may sometimes appear friendly. Do not be misled. A coyote—any wild animal—that attempts to cozy up to a rockhound (even to an ordinary human) is rowing with only one oar in the water. Throw rocks, throw sticks, fire a gun, use strong language to discourage such a critter. You will be glad you did.

The Abert's squirrel is one of two tufted-ear squirrels found in Arizona.

Everything said about the coyote applies equally to other desert predators, such as the bobcat, the fox, and the mountain lion. Even though these three are mostly night hunters seldom seen during daylight, one that acts sick or friendly should be sent packing.

Many Arizona rockhound collecting locales house a decent population of reptiles. Nearly all are harmless to humans, or nearly so. A few, under rare conditions, can inflict pain and suffering. The most obvious example is the rattlesnake. Eleven species of rattlesnakes can be found in Arizona, ranging from the robust western diamondback, up to five feet long, to the petite 1.5-foot massasauga. The nature of snakes and the nature of rockhounds can cause occasional confrontations. A bite might occur in a small percentage of those confrontations. Current wisdom suggests that a person who has been bitten by a rattlesnake, or a snake suspected to be a rattlesnake, should seek medical help immediately.

Two other potentially dangerous reptiles are the coral snake and the gila monster. Both are brightly colored and are somewhat slow-moving. The rare bites reported almost always occur as the human attempts to tease or manipulate the reptile.

Do not let the fear of snakes, lizards, and other critters diminish your enjoyment of the Arizona outdoors. Human/critter confrontations are rare. Knowing a bit about the wildlife you might encounter, however, can lead you to be particularly careful as you collect.

DESERT TRAVEL

Arizona is a land of wide-open spaces—the wild and wooly West. Much of the state is low desert. Another big chunk is the slightly higher terrain called the Sonoran Desert. In both, the land is essentially dry. Although scattered stock tanks contain enough water to permit cattle to survive, this water is seldom fit for human consumption. Summer temperatures throughout most of the two deserts reach temperatures considerably higher than 100 degrees Fahrenheit. Nighttime temperatures are less hot: It can chill off way down to ninety or so. Smart desert denizens turn nocturnal to survive. Smart rockhounds avoid the area between about May 15 and October 1. Here are seven tips that can make your desert adventure worry-free:

1. DO NOT ATTEMPT BACKCOUNTRY TRAVEL IN AN INADEQUATE VEHICLE. The sheer size of the Arizona wild country creates a hazard. A semi-simple mechanical problem, one that would scarcely cause a worry on the freeway, can furrow the brow with worry lines as deep as the Grand Canyon. A ruptured radiator hose, or a broken fan belt, for example, can cause a heap of trouble if you happen to be forty or fifty miles from help. Passenger cars seldom have the muscle and clearance needed to negotiate primitive roads. A pickup truck is better and a pickup truck equipped with four-wheel drive and a winch is best. Even so, experienced desert trekkers carry spare parts for emergency repairs.

2. TELL A RELATIVE, A FRIEND, EVEN AN ENEMY IF NO ONE ELSE IS AVAILABLE, YOUR DESTINATION AND ANTICIPATED RETURN DATE. Doing so will give the search and rescue folks an advantage when they come looking for you. Having imparted travel and return plans, STICK TO THEM. Nothing makes an S&R guy madder than saddling up to rescue a dude who is not in trouble.

3. CARRY SUFFICIENT WATER. The human body requires water on a regular basis and requires quite a lot of it. Carry a minimum of one gallon of water a day for each of the folks in your party.

4. WEAR SENSIBLE CLOTHING. Loose-fitting trousers or slacks and a long-sleeved shirt or blouse are sensible. So is a wide-brimmed hat, one that will screen out most of the sun's harmful rays. Carry a high-grade sun screen to apply to areas that remain exposed. The desert sun, even in winter, can change a pale face into a red face in one hell of a hurry.

5. CARRY AN EMERGENCY SUPPLY OF FOOD. Canned vegetables, canned fruit, even canned tuna can taste mighty good in the event of a breakdown.

6. STAY WITH THE VEHICLE. Search and rescue professionals sug-

gest that you stay with the vehicle until rescued. The vehicle is easy to spot from the air, whereas a person afoot is not.

7. WHEN STUCK IN THE SAND, clear the sand away from the tires and lay vegetation within the ruts. If all else fails, remove about half of the air from the tires. The semi-flat aspect will provide better traction that sometimes allows escape.

Planning and preparation are the keys to safe a collecting trip in Arizona, just as everywhere. The remoteness of some collecting sites, however, makes it more critical. Thousands of rockers visit Arizona collecting sites yearly, and nearly all do so without problems.

Rockhound roads often lead into remote country. A breakdown here can spell serious trouble.

ROCKHOUND RULES

Much of the Copper State's land is publicly owned, land that is managed by state and federally funded land managers. Much is managed to encourage multiple uses. Cattle grazing, timber harvesting, hunting, fishing, trapping, camping, and rockhounding often are allowed. Each land manager has formulated access regulations that enhance the provisions of their purview. A list of major land managers follows, along with a brief list of important regulations as they apply to rockhound use.

BUREAU OF LAND MANAGEMENT

Nearly all Bureau of Land Management (BLM) land within the state is under lease to livestock grazing, primarily cattle, and to a lesser degree, sheep. A grazing lease allows a rancher to graze a certain number of livestock for a fee. It buys no other proprietorship. The land remains open to all other lawful and legitimate uses.

A unwritten law in the West requires visitors on leased land to show a degree of common courtesy. Close all gates that you find closed. Leave open gates that you find open. Do not attempt to camp around stock tanks or other stock and game watering structures. To do so will cause livestock and wild game to go without water. And it's against the law.

BLM regulations allow you to remove rocks, minerals, and some fossils from BLM lands. Fossils of unusual importance are excepted. Vertebrate fossils are considered protected. Invertebrate fossils, for the most part, can be legally collected. Fossilized wood may be collected, but the booty is limited to twenty-five pounds per day, per individual, with a yearly limit of 250 pounds. All regulations cited pertain to hobby collecting. Commercial collecting, where allowed, is controlled by separate regulations.

Artifacts may not be removed from BLM land without a specific permit, and only legitimate scientific organizations receive permits. The Federal Antiquities Act of 1906 specifies that such artifacts are part of the scientific history of our civilization, and as such, must remain within the public domain. That means no collecting of arrowheads, spearpoints, metates, manos, or even pottery shards. In fact, this law applies to all public and federal lands. Such collecting, it is assumed, can continue on private property if you obtain owner permission.

The BLM offers for sale a series of maps that can be immensely helpful to the rock and mineral hound. Even though most are sadly outdated, they retain good information about mountain ranges, drainages, and other some-what constant geological phenomena. Each map covers eighty townships (about 3,000 square miles) and shows ownership status of much of the land. Major and minor roadways, as they were at the time of mapping, also are shown.

The Federal Antiquities Act of 1906 makes it illegal to collect artifacts from public lands.

NATIONAL FORESTS

Much of Arizona is within the domain of one of the numerous national forests located within the state. Every forest publishes a map that lists geologic features such as mountains, streams, lakes, and even stock ponds. Forest roads are numbered to facilitate travel. The information is almost always current. The maps can be purchased at most national forest headquarters at a moderate cost.

As noted, the U.S.D.A. Forest Service is bound by the Federal Antiquities Act of 1906 and enforces its provisions. Rock, mineral, and fossil collecting for hobby purposes is generally permitted on Forest Service land, just as it is on BLM land.

The national forests within Arizona (a list is included) offer an excellent opportunity for recreation: rockhounding, of course. Improved campgrounds offer camping sites, and streams and lakes, stocked with trout, offer summer fishing. Photographers will find that many of the forests teem with wildlife, such as elk, deer, pronghorn, bear, lion, turkey, and numerous others. Hunting is allowed in season.

STATE TRUST LANDS

State trust lands are almost always identified by a sign advising that entry is prohibited without proper permit. A valid hunting or fishing license, an attorney general's ruling has decided, allows access to the holder. A permit can be purchased from any State Land Office that allows rockhound entry.

Casual collecting of rocks, minerals, and fossils has been permitted in the past. Laws that control removal of state land resources, however, are poorly understood. It is best to contact a state trust land representative if your travels take you to a part of the state trust holdings.

TRIBAL LANDS

Each of Arizona's fifteen tribal reservations is autonomous, that is, each tribal government establishes access regulations for its reservation. Consult the list of reservations elsewhere in this book for current addresses and phone numbers.

PRIVATE PROPERTY

You must have owner permission to collect on posted private property within Arizona. Many of the seemingly abandoned mining operations are posted against trespass. Common courtesy, common sense, and the law require you to respect the posting. If the area appears to be open to public access and no posting is present, some collectors assume tacit permission. Even so, if at all possible, make an effort to determine ownership and obtain permission to enter.

Even with owner permission, keep in mind that mines, mine workings, and mine dumps can be a hazardous place to collect. Common sense can keep you safe.

Many petroglyphs depict animals, such as these deer figures found near Fossil Creek Springs.

ARIZONA'S MINERAL HIGHLIGHTS

PETROGLYPHS AND PICTOGRAPHS

A hobbyist who spends much time trekking the Arizona backcountry is sure to encounter an example of prehistoric rock writing. This message from the past can be of two general types, petroglyphs or pictographs. Petroglyphs are designs pecked into a rock surface. The rocks chosen were often black-stained, colored by a process that produces a desert varnish. The pecking, usually with a pointed rock used as a chisel and a rounded rock as a hammer, exposed the lighter interior of the rock.

Pictographs are similar designs painted onto a protected rock surface, sometimes on undercut cliffs, sometimes in caves. The "paint" was a mixture of pulverized mineral pigment (limonite stained sandstone was popular) mixed with urine or blood. The finger, in all probability, was the applicator.

Writings of both types, and all other prehistoric evidence, are protected by state and federal antiquity laws. Observe, photograph, but do not attempt to collect or deface. You would destroy an important link to the past. And if apprehended, you would face a stiff fine and perhaps imprisonment.

Two particularly fine examples of petroglyphs within Arizona are easily accessible. One is the Newspaper Rock area within the Petrified Forest National Park. Newspaper Rock is an immense cliff section that is nearly filled with anthropomorphic and zoomorphic peckings. In some areas of the rock, newer peckings cover older work. The cliff faces that surround Newspaper Rock and nearby caves also have interesting petroglyphs.

The second example of petroglyphs occurs within Painted Rock State Park twenty-six miles north of Interstate 8, near the town of Gila Bend. The park is located to the west of Painted Rocks Dam and the lake above. Do not plan to fish the lake. The waters have a high saline content and also are polluted by upstream pesticides.

Pictographs are less common than petroglyphs. The best example within the state is the pictographs found in Snake Canyon (yep, there are snakes there) on the north Kaibab. The paintings here are humanoids of heroic size—some to ten feet. Several of the well-articulated figures show antennae, a feature that has caused some to speculate that they represent beings from outer space.

Although a passable road runs the length of Snake Gulch, the area is a designated wilderness area, so those who hanker for a look at the pictographs must hike about ten miles to the site. A second example of pictographs is found in a cave within Petrified Forest National Park, in a roadless area a mile or two east of the Rio Puerco Ruins. Most images on the low ceiling are of human handprints. The makers apparently wet their hands with a limonite paint and pressed them firmly to the ceiling to produce an imprint. The size of the hands indicates small individuals, perhaps women or young men.

ARIZONA TURQUOISE

Turquoise is a byproduct of the copper mining industry in Arizona. Four open pit operations have yielded nearly all of the Arizona turquoise on the market. Currently, two of the four are inactive. Much of the turquoise produced by the two active mines is a low-grade material called chalk. The lack of color and hardness of this low grade causes it to be unattractive to lapidaries, but several firms treat the chalky material to "enhance" or "stabilize" it. The chalk is heated to cause it to throw off moisture and is then impregnated with hot acrylic. The resultant product is handsome and somewhat hard.

The Duval property at Ithaca Peak almost surely deserves the crown as the premiere turquoise-producing property in the state. Located thirty miles northwest of Kingman, just off U.S. 93, the peak was mined for turquoise by aboriginal people. In more modern times, the deposit was an underground operation and finally was turned into the more economical open pit operation.

Most of the turquoise was found during the early days of the pit. Huge machines stripped off the overburden to expose the copper-bearing porphyry. The stripping of the overburden uncovered massive veins of turquoise—tons of turquoise.

The quality of the Ithaca Peak turquoise varied radically, just as it does in nearly every occurrence. Much was chalky and required stabilization before it would be attractive to the jewelry trade. A good part was hard enough and blue enough to be used untreated. A small percentage was high grade—some of it spiderwebbed and some of it an electric blue that dazzled the eye—as good a any turquoise available.

Foreign and domestic buyers flocked to Kingman to purchase their share of the bounty. The peak of production coincided with the turquoise/Indian jewelry phenomena of the late 1970s and early 1980s. Many tons of "Kingman turquoise" traveled to faraway firms in Germany, Japan, and other lands.

Duval shut down the Ithaca Peak property because of low copper prices and labor negotiations during the early 1980s. Turquoise continues to be mined on a somewhat casual basis by lessees. Check with rockshops and rockhounds in the Kingman area to find a source of treated and untreated material.

The Lavender Pit at Bisbee, a Phelps Dodge operation, is a second property that has closed because of depressed copper prices and high labor costs. During the days of operation, Bisbee produced a hard, deep blue turquoise that sometimes occurred in a hard red (cuprite?) matrix. This beautiful turquoise, the famous Bisbee Blue, was immediately coveted by cutters and collectors. Even though some casual collecting of the dumps continues, the quantity of turquoise recovered is commercially insignificant. Hobbyists

Turquoise miners collect from a seam uncovered at Duval's Ithaca Peak property.

who hanker for a piece of natural or treated Bisbee turquoise are advised to visit local rock shops and to contact local rockhounds. Check with the Chamber of Commerce to learn meeting dates of local rockhound clubs. Go as a guest. Take some material from home along as trading bait. You may be glad you did.

The Sleeping Beauty property south of Miami has been a steady producer of turquoise for many years. The best quality is a medium blue seam turquoise. Nearly all of the material is without inclusions, and most of it is hard and fracture-free.

As is the case with other Arizona turquoise, some of the Sleeping Beauty production is soft and pale. Much is locally enhanced and stabilized. Find the turquoise as you would within other communities. Check rockshops and make contact with local rockhounds in the nearby communities of Miami and Globe.

The final important Arizona turquoise producer is the open pit property located at Morenci. Ravaged by union riots during the 80s, the Morenci pit is currently operating with a reduced workforce. Turquoise collecting rights continue to be leased. Production is sporadic, increasing as important seams of turquoise are exposed. Morenci turquoise varies considerably in quality. Some is soft and needs enhancement to be attractive to the lapidary. At the high end of the scale, the turquoise is hard and a flawless blue. At other times the top grade will show an intricate spider webbing. Collectors seeking Morenci turquoise are advised to try rockshops within the towns of Clifton and Safford, both south of the pit on U.S. 666. Make it a point to visit the Brown Brothers Lapidary at Safford. As you would do in other turquoise locales, attend a meeting of the local rockhound club to make contact with locals.

Many other copper properties within Arizona have produced turquoise occasionally, but none have produced turquoise in a quality or quantity to deserve mention.

SILICA IMPREGNATED CHRYSOCOLLA

Chrysocolla, the mineral, is a disappointing lapidary material. The low Mohs ranking (2.4) makes the material too soft for most gemstone applications. At surface humidity, the material loses water and turns brittle. Add silica as a chrysocolla constituent, however, and the material changes dramatically. Silica-impregnated chrysocolla might be the most beautiful and most desirable of the many elite gemstones found within the state. And when you say that, you might just as well say in the world.

Chrysocolla silicate was probably formed as percolating groundwater rich in silica collected fine grains of the complex copper called chrysocolla. The fortuitous marriage was precipitated out as a hard and glassy gem rock.

Silica impregnated chrysocolla is hard, blue, and rare. The material is not well known to even experienced lapidaries. Those few who have found and worked the material, however, have immediately recognized the superior qualities of this rare copper silica. Like other chalcedonies, the material ranks high on the Mohs scale (7.5). The material accepts an excellent polish and is a durable gemstone. Silica impregnated chrysocolla (or vice versa) is almost exclusively a byproduct of the Arizona mining industry. The best quality found, in all probability, came from a generous vein within the Live Oak Shaft of the Miami Inspiration Mine. The late Walter Haught of Payson, Arizona, worked there during the early 1920s. During a conversation held in the mid-60s, Mr. Haught recalled that a huge body of glassy blue chalcedony was encountered at the 500-foot level. Specimens of the blue glass as large as washtubs were found. There were few lapidaries then, and sadly, nearly all of the material went to the waste dump with the rest of the gangue (worthless rock). Later, as the mine turned from shaft and tunnel to pit, and as smelting processes improved to handle ore rich in silica, the dump was mined and the blue glass was destroyed for the copper content.

The copper silica found within the Miami Inspiration Mine was sometimes a deep sky blue with no inclusions. Other specimens showed an intergrowth of the copper carbonate malachite. On rare occasions, the silica was colored an electric blue by inclusions of the copper carbonate azurite.

Other Arizona mines produced gem quality chrysocolla. The Cyprus Mines property at Bagdad, Arizona, comes immediately to mind. Some Bagdad material has bright red inclusions of the copper oxide cuprite within the glassy blue silicate. Other specimens show a splendent druse of quartz over a colorful layer of chrysocolla. Other specimens had native copper as

This hand-sized chunk of chrysocolla-colored chalcedony came from a seam discovered in 1930 at the Live Oak Shaft near Miami.

over a colorful layer of chrysocolla. Other specimens had native copper as inclusions within the chrysocolla.

The most striking cabochon of chrysocolla extant, in all probability, can be found within the collection owned by Martin Koning of Morristown, Arizona. The fist-sized chunk showed the typical glassy blue field. Within, liberated by the diamond saw, was a series of wormlike inclusions of bright red cuprite. Although the source of the specimen is not documented, it likely came from the workings at Bagdad, a place where the silica-chrysocolla-cuprite combination has been found.

Rockhounds seeking to own a piece of this most beautiful of coppers must employ the silver pick. Rockshops located within mining towns can be one source. Miners who "lunchbox" out jewelry rock can be another. In either case, look for material that is glassy and colorful. Touching the tip of the tongue (the rockhound salute) to the material can be helpful in determining hardness. If the tongue sticks to the rock, denoting a thirst for water, the material is not likely to be hard enough for lapidary use.

Chrysocolla-silicate should be worked wet. The material is heat-sensitive (even more so than other chalcedonies). Too much heat can cause a conchoidal fracture along the edge or a partial fracture within the interior. Too much heat can cause the color to fade. Work the material wet through the 320 grit wheel. Wet sand through the 600 grit wheel. Polish, using tin or chrome oxide on rough leather. Take the time needed to produce a flawless finish. Moderate to heavy pressure can somewhat hasten the polishing

THAR'S GOLD IN THEM THAR HILLS

Hopeful prospectors combed nearly every dry wash in Arizona during the late 1870s and early 1880s. Each had a common goal, and that goal was GOLD.

Most prospectors found their mine by following a tedious but effective procedure. They would meticulously inspect washes and gullies to find a trace of the yellow metal. They would pan the sand and powder rock specimens to search out gold content. Knowing that rock can only travel downhill, any promising color was followed uphill until the source was discovered.

A few of the gold properties carry a more romantic legend. The Vulture Mine was discovered when Henry Wickenburg flung a rock at an errant burro. The rock split open upon impact (with the ground, not the burro) to expose visible gold.

A party of gold seekers organized by A.H. Peeples combed the hills fifteen miles to the east of the present-day town of Congress. A member of the party climbed to a hilltop (Rich Hill) and discovered surface gold. More than a half-million dollars in gold nuggets were picked from the surface.

Where did the gold come from? Geologists believe that the gold came from the erosion of a granite that contained many rich veinlets of gold. To this day, after a hard rain, a lucky collector might find a gold nugget upon the flat mesa top called Rich Hill.

The immense granite batholith called the Bradshaw Mountain Range has yielded up mind-boggling quantities of gold. Rich Hill, described above, is one such. Others, only slightly less rich, grace every aspect of the range.

Modern prospectors follow streambeds to search for "colors."

Current collectors retrieve the placer gold in one of two general ways, panning, a process that requires water, and dry-washing, a process that requires copious amounts of sweat. Both panners and dry-washers use essentially the same technique to locate a likely spot. They visit areas that have produced gold in the past to search the sands of dry washes for signs of mineralization. The most consistent indicator is the black sand (magnetite) that is associated with gold in many instances. Black sand areas, much of the time, will yield up a bit of gold.

A third gold-hunting technique, increasingly popular, involves the use of metal detection devices. Some of these electronic marvels are so sophisticated they can discern the presence of a copper penny (even those of recent manufacture that hold a minimal amount of copper) down to a depth of a foot or two.

The gold hunters of the last century searched mostly for lode gold. There were no dry-washers and no metal detectors available. The nuggets and flour gold of the dry washes went mainly unmolested. Much of it remains to this day, waiting for the right combination of work, skill, and luck to free it from its rocky hideout.

DESERT IRONWOOD

Desert ironwood (*Olneya tesota* Gray) is a super-hard member of the legume family. The dead wood carries a specific gravity of 1.14. A cubic foot of this beautifully patterned wood will weigh sixty-six pounds, exceeded in density only by the leadwood found in Florida. Southwestern jewelers use slabs and slices of desert ironwood as a jewelry component. Some cut out a large cab of the wood and use it as a base for silver cutouts. Others saw fine channels into the wood and inlay silver wire to construct an animal likeness. Still others add bits of the wood with colorful gemstone to make an inlay or mosaic of unusual beauty.

The tough and tenacious nature of the wood makes it impervious to ordinary saws and axes. A chainsaw will cut the ironwood logs into manageable chunks, but the teeth of the chain will require frequent sharpening. A table saw or a radial arm saw equipped with a carbide-tipped blade does a decent job of slabbing.

Desert ironwood can be worked on the lapidary unit. It is best to work wet to control excessive dust. Finish the cabochon just as you would a semisoft gemstone, on a used 600-grit cloth. Some hobbyists apply a coating of cordovan wax shoe polish as a final finish.

Most of the ironwood areas are under the jurisdiction of the Bureau of Land Management (BLM). Each BLM region sets rules for the collection of woods within the region. A spokesman for the Maricopa County Region (Phoenix) states that there is no "hobby" permit available to allow the collecting of desert ironwood. There is, however, a firewood collecting permit available ($10.00 for one cord), and dead desert ironwood is not excluded.

Much of the desert land west of Phoenix to the California border (Colorado

Above: *Dead desert ironwood can be collected if the proper permits are obtained.* **Left:** *Desert ironwood serves as a beautiful background for silver cutouts, including this image of Kokopelli.*

River) is habitat suitable to desert ironwood needs. The ironwood shares space, much of the time, with another legume, the true mesquite. The skeletons of the trees can appear similar. To find the dead ironwood, look along dry washes (desert waterways that are wet only during runoff). The exterior of the dead ironwood will be a deep brown-red and will almost always have a textured, "sandblasted" aspect.

Some Southwest Indians, such as the Seri of Sonora Mexico, carve desert ironwood into quail, ducks, and even bighorn sheep to sell to tourists.

All of the ironwood habitat is hot during the summer—too hot for comfort or safety. You should schedule collecting trips for the winter months, after you obtain the proper permits. A four-wheel-drive vehicle will be an asset, because much of the best material is located along remote and primitive roads.

ROCKHOUND CONVENTIONS AND GEM SHOWS

QUARTZSITE POW WOW

Quartzsite, Arizona, correctly can be called the Rockhound Capital of Arizona (maybe the whole durned world) during the month of February. Thousands of recreational vehicles gather here to participate in the annual pow wow. Hundreds of visitors bring rocks, gems, jewelry, and even minerals to sell or trade to other rockhounds. Often the asking price is surprisingly modest.

Many of the February folks, it should be noted, travel to Quartzsite many months before—around the first of November when the mild winter begins. The land that surrounds this small community is administered by the federal Bureau of Land Management. Visitors who own self-contained recreational vehicles often spend the winter here—snowbirds fleeing the frigid climate of their home states. Long-term camping is permitted at no charge or upon payment of a modest recreational fee.

Visitors who hope to see the entire pow wow should schedule a minimum of three or four days. There are many hundreds of tailgate dealers. Seeing everything may require a walk of a mile or more. Here are tips that might make the viewing more enjoyable: Wear sensible shoes. The amount of

This hematite/quartz cooperation was found near Quartzsite.

Manufacturers also display their wares at the Quartzsite Pow Wow every February.

walking required can make the dogs howl. Wear loose-fitting clothing that adequately covers arms and legs. Apply a good grade of sunscreen to exposed skin. The winter sun can spot an eastern paleface in a New York minute. Carry a stout bag to hold the booty. Carry cash or traveler's checks—many tailgaters will not accept charge cards or personal checks.

If you develop a hankering to lease tailgate space of your very own—maybe sell a bit of the excess from your collection—you should know that more than one show is held within the Quartzsite area during mid-winter. The oldest and the best attended is the Quartzsite Pow Wow sponsored by the Quartzsite Improvement Association. The 1992 effort was the QIA's twenty-sixth annual show. More than 500 dealers participated. The show traditionally starts the first Wednesday in February. Contact The Quartzsite Improvement Association, Box 881, Quartzsite, AZ 85346, for information on space.

The annual Tyson Wells Sell-A-Rama is a ten-day doing that usually begins the last day of January. Contact Lloyd Dyer at (602) 927-6364 for space information. Cloud's Jamboree begins about the middle of January and runs until about the middle of February. Contact Dick Cloud at P.O. Box 1917, Quartzsite, AZ 85346, (602) 927-6334 for show and space information.

If you are RVing to Quartzsite, stock the camper with adequate supplies of water and foodstuffs. Camping space is sometimes available at unimproved campgrounds and is always available out on the desert. In either case, your camper should be self-contained. Quartzsite during "the doings" is an experience every rockhound should enjoy at least once. Often, a single visit can cause a yearly return, perhaps to spend the winter.

TUCSON GEM AND MINERAL SHOW

Dan Caudle, Clayton Gibson, and the late Harold Ruper held the first Tucson Gem and Mineral Show in a school auditorium. The year was 1955. That modest exhibition has grown to be the most important gem and mineral show in the world. Rock and mineral hounds fly and drive (some may even hitchhike) from nearly every country to participate in the affair collectors have come to call "Tucson."

The Tucson show is held annually during the second weekend of February at the spacious Tucson Community Center. Satellite shows take place within many local motels. Dealers, denied space at the main show, take over entire floors, and sometimes, entire hotels and motels, to display their wares. The satellites, almost always, come early and stay late, timing their stay to include the show, and a period of time before and after the show. Attendance at the show was listed at 26,850 in 1988.

The show organizer (Tucson Gem & Mineral Society) began a popular feature in 1960 when they asked Paul Desautels to attend and display an exhibit from the Smithsonian. Important collections, both public and private, are displayed at every show.

The Tucson Community Center is in downtown Tucson. Pay parking is available off Church Street south of Broadway. Admission is $2, with children under 14 admitted free. If you hope to stay at one of Tucson's hotels or motels during "Show Week," you must make reservations early. Some hotel/motels are fully booked a year in advance.

Part of the show, and some satellite shows, are restricted to properly licensed gem, gemstone, and mineral dealers. If you intend to visit the wholesale shows, you must bring along the proper credentials.

February weather in Tucson is almost always great. Daytime highs register about 70 degrees, cooling at night. Bring a set or two of comfortable walking shoes (you will do a lot of it) and a sweater or windbreaker. Contact the Metropolitan Tucson Convention and Visitors Bureau (602) 624-1817, or the Tucson Metropolitan Chamber of Commerce (602) 792-2250, for further information.

ROCKHOUNDING SITES IN ARIZONA

The remains of the United Verde Hotel, which once housed miners, now stand sentinel over abandoned equipment at the diggings.

SITE 1: *THE UNITED VERDE MINE*

The year 1894 brought good news and bad news to the United Verde Mine at Jerome. The good news was production. Eleven million pounds of copper and 300 tons of silver were smelted. The bad news? The sulphide ore body deep underground caught fire and burned tenaciously for more than thirty years. That fire cooperated with the pyritic ore to produce a secondary suite of mineralization. Much within that suite of minerals was rare to the point of uniqueness—found nowhere else in the world.

The underground fire began when part of the sulphide ore body slipped to cause fire-starting friction. Choking clouds of sulphuric smoke and a tunnel temperature of 150 degrees Fahrenheit caused miners to claim it was like "being in hell itself." Fire minerals such as digenite, ransomite, roemerite, lausenite, coquimbite, butlerite, guildite, and copiapite were formed.

Historically, Spanish explorers had visited the black hills of the area about 1583. Verde Valley Indians took them to "the Cave of the Blue Rock." Stone tools at the entrance to the short tunnel indicated the blue rock had been mined for pigment and jewelry rock for hundreds of years. Because the ore was obviously mainly copper, the Spanish lost interest. About 300 years later

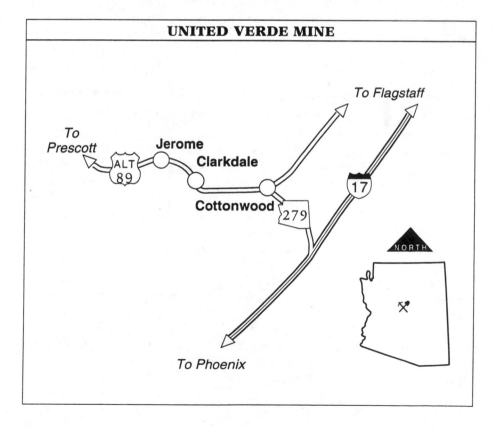

UNITED VERDE MINE

a pair of prospectors filed claim to the outcropping. The mine eventually came to be owned by Senator William A. Clark of Montana, and the mine was developed as the United Verde.

Even though he was an experienced mining man, Clark did not lay claim to a fractional part of a nearby claim. A local merchant quickly filed a claim and called it the Little Daisy. In later years this small piece of ground provided access to a split-off portion of the United Verde ore body. Now named the United Verde Extension (UVX), it gave up $125 million. The mine was eventually sold to Phelps Dodge and was mined until 1947. Six hundred million dollars in copper had been taken from the ore body. Eight hundred tons of silver and twenty-eight tons of gold sweetened the pot.

The mines of Cleopatra Hill are still now. The town of Jerome bills itself as a ghost town, but it is not. Several hundred hardy residents continue to occupy the houses that hug the hillside. A full-time care taker is on site to prevent trespass into the dangerous depths of the Phelps Dodge Pit.

Even though no collecting is allowed, much here will interest the rock and mineral collector. The mine museum offers a look at relics from the mines. The Phelps Dodge Pit (sometimes called The Big Hole) was the first open pit operation in Arizona. Mostly inactive, the Phelps Dodge Corporation sometimes leases limited mining rights to smaller companies. When this happens, a dribble of mineral specimens, mostly crystalline azurite, becomes available. The Douglas Memorial Mining Museum, part of the Arizona State Park system, provides a look at much of the machinery used to extract and refine the ore. Part of the park offers a look at mineral specimens from the area.

SITE 2: *MINING AND MINERALS AT BAGDAD*

Even though the Bagdad copper property was located in 1880 (by John Lawler), the area's remoteness caused it to be largely ignored until about the late 1930s. The surface ore at this property sixty-five miles west of Prescott was low grade. The property endured a series of ownerships, none of them profitable. The beginning of World War II boosted the demand for strategic metals. Bagdad prospered, as did most other mines within the state.

The post-war owners determined that the Bagdad orebody was not structured for efficient underground mining. Thus, underground mining ended here in 1950 and an efficient open pit operation began. An on-site mill processed 4,500 tons of ore each day. The concentrate was hauled by truck to the nearest railhead at Hillside.

Bagdad has been a stingy, but steady, producer of minerals and cuttables for the hobbyist. The best of the true cuttables was likely the glassy blue chrysocolla-impregnated silica that sometimes contained bold red flashes of cuprite, or less commonly, inclusions of native copper. A close second would

The Bagdad Pit has produced fine specimens of chrysocolla, malachite, chalcotrichite, and native copper

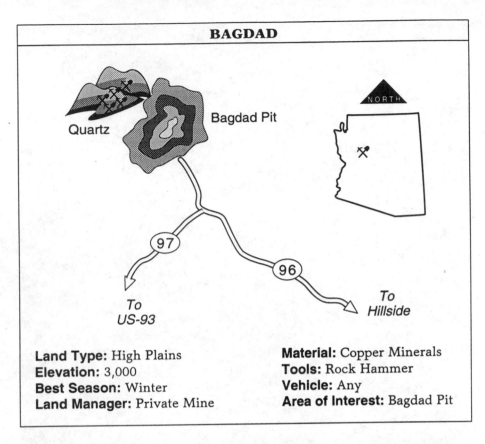

BAGDAD

Quartz

Bagdad Pit

NORTH

97

96

To
US-93

To
Hillside

Land Type: High Plains
Elevation: 3,000
Best Season: Winter
Land Manager: Private Mine

Material: Copper Minerals
Tools: Rock Hammer
Vehicle: Any
Area of Interest: Bagdad Pit

be the quartz druse, stained a brilliant blue by enclosed chrysocolla, which coated some cavities of the ore and the gangue. A cuttable malachite/chrysocolla mixture, while crumbly, could be cut into eye-catching cabs.

The high desert hills that surround this remote mine are loaded with potential for the rockhound. The author collected at a hill just west of the Bagdad Pit (properly called the Cyprus-Bagdad Pit) during the late 1960s and found a number of interesting crystallizations of quartz (some specimens showed Japan Twinning). Some specimens consisted of a glassy red jasper containing imbedded quartz crystals. An abandoned mine east of the mine, and east of Boulder Creek, offers up decent specimens of pyrite within quartz.

The Bagdad Mine currently operates. On occasion the owners offer tours to interested groups. In the past, they have dumped a truckload or two of colorful rock at the lip of the pit so that collectors might pick through to find a specimen or two.

SITE 3: *MAGMA MINE*

The Magma Mine at Superior is not known to be a specimen mine. The underground miners here go about the serious job of mining copper, their tedium seldom disturbed by a crystal find. Collectors who bypass Superior because of this reputation, however, may be missing a bet. Crystal pockets are sometimes found within the depths of the Magma Mine (formerly called the Silver Queen). And those pockets can yield up specimens that will dazzle the eye of the most discriminating collector

The barite find of the mid-1970s is a good example. Miners were surprised when they entered the chalcocite ore body to find a series of mud-filled cavities, some as large as a #2 washtub. The miners were even more surprised when they discovered stout and sharply terminated crystals hidden away in the desiccated mud. The crystals, some singles and some clusters, showed a black or brown splendent face when clean. A few were glass clear and were a beautiful gold color. A mine geologist made the identification. The crystals were barite and were possibly the most attractive specimens of that material found. Dealers and collectors flocked to the area to haggle lunch box quantities from the miners.

A second series of pockets yielded up handsome crystals of a different

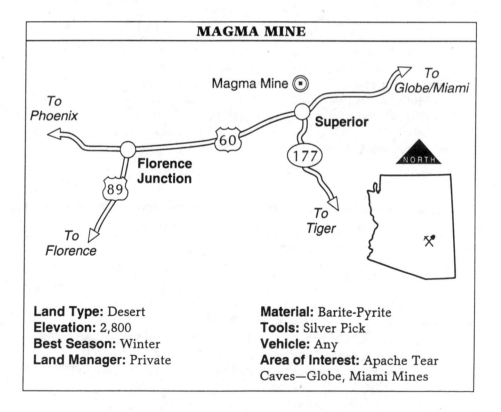

MAGMA MINE

To Phoenix

Magma Mine ⊙

To Globe/Miami

Superior

60

Florence Junction

177

89

To Tiger

To Florence

NORTH

Land Type: Desert
Elevation: 2,800
Best Season: Winter
Land Manager: Private

Material: Barite-Pyrite
Tools: Silver Pick
Vehicle: Any
Area of Interest: Apache Tear Caves—Globe, Miami Mines

An intrusive mud protected superb specimens of black, brown, and gold barite

kind—clusters of gold-colored pyrite with some individual crystal faces exceeding two inches. The clusters were clean and splendent. The few specimens found quickly disappeared into local collections.

It has been two decades since the barite/pyrite find. Other minor crystal pockets have been encountered since. Rockhounds who visit the area to collect the nearby Apache Tear Caves might be well rewarded if they take the time to attend a meeting of the local rock and mineral club. Talk to service station attendants and folks who work in the grocery store. Many of them will have relatives who work at the mine. **The mine is off limits to the public**, but you may be able to use the "silver pick" to obtain a prized specimen for your collection.

SITE 4: *VANADINITE AT THE APACHE MINE*

The vanadium property, located a few miles northwest of Miami, enjoyed a brief period of productivity during the World War II years. The ore, mostly in the form of brilliant and blood red vanadinite crystals, was used to harden and toughen steel.

The workings, at the time of the author's last visit (about 1970), consisted of a badly weathered shaft that provided access to about a hundred feet or so. Landings, some accessing tunnels and stopes, were located at about every twenty feet. Many of the tunnels that led to the stopes had caved. A skinny person (author was somewhat so at the time) who had a complete lack of common sense could traverse these slides by lying on his or her back, sucking in the breath, and scrooching along a barely big enough crawl space.

The vanadinite occurred in chimneys of fractured rock. The crystals, up to matchhead size, were mostly a deep and splendent red, grading to a pale yellow. Some of the crystal specimens showed vanadinite associated with mottramite, calcite, or quartz crystals. The Apache Mine vanadinites, if only color is considered, are likely the finest examples of the lead vanadate found so far.

The Apache Mine workings are not accessible as this is written. Crystal miners sometimes attempt recovery by open pit mining and offer the booty through rock shops in the Globe/Miami area. The John Mediz shop in Globe is a good source for Apache Mine vanadinite, minerals from the Seventy-nine Mine, and copper cuttables and minerals from the Miami-Inspiration pit.

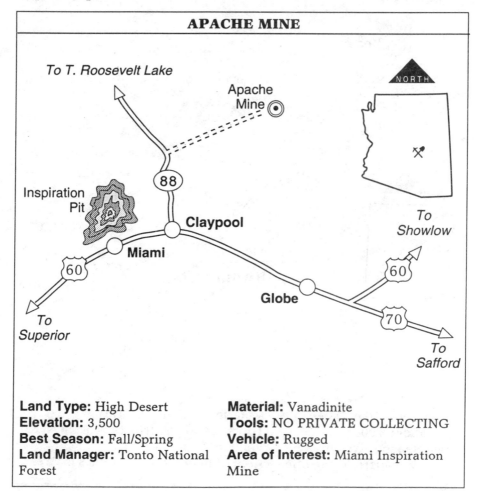

APACHE MINE

Land Type: High Desert	**Material:** Vanadinite
Elevation: 3,500	**Tools:** NO PRIVATE COLLECTING
Best Season: Fall/Spring	**Vehicle:** Rugged
Land Manager: Tonto National Forest	**Area of Interest:** Miami Inspiration Mine

SITE 5: *THE SEVENTY-NINE MINE*

The Seventy-nine Mine was located by Mike and Pat O'Brien in 1879. (Maybe that's why they call it the Seventy-nine?) Deep within the Dripping Springs Mountains, the ore was transported on burro back to the railhead at Hayden Junction. Primarily a lead property, the mine's ore also contained values in gold, silver, and copper. The Seventy-nine suffered through a series of ownerships, nearly all unprofitable. As is the case with most lead properties within the state, more money was poured into the ground than ever came out. The last significant activity at the mine began during 1940.

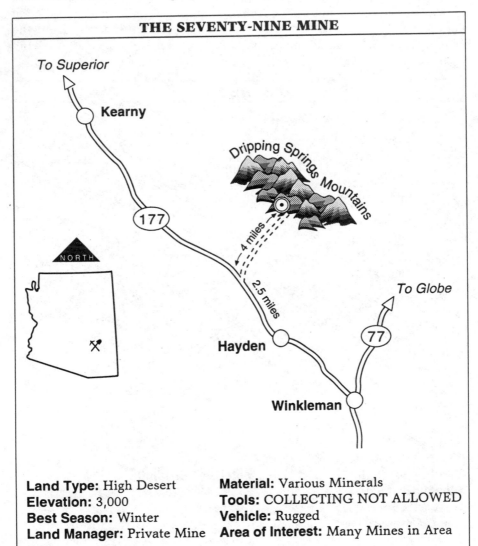

THE SEVENTY-NINE MINE

To Superior

Kearny

Dripping Springs Mountains

177

4 miles

2.5 miles

To Globe

77

Hayden

Winkleman

Land Type: High Desert
Elevation: 3,000
Best Season: Winter
Land Manager: Private Mine

Material: Various Minerals
Tools: COLLECTING NOT ALLOWED
Vehicle: Rugged
Area of Interest: Many Mines in Area

The Shattuck-Denn Mining Corporation spent a pile of money, eventually descending to the 700-foot level. The work was exploratory and the results were disappointing. The company remained active through the war years and ceased operations in 1949.

The Seventy-nine was, and is, one of the premier specimen mines of the West. The combination of lead and copper within the limestone gangue has cooperated to produce fine crystallizations of wulfenite, rosasite, hemimorphite, and others. The wulfenite occurs as fragile and transparent splendent yellow crystals up to two inches across. The rosasite specimens occur as closely clustered hairs of a handsome green-blue. The

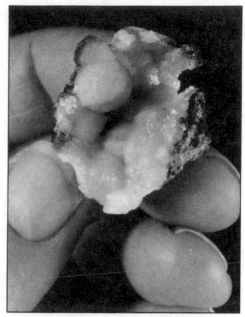

A large seam of blue hemimorphite was found deep underground at the Seventy-nine mine.

hemimorphite is crusty and non-crystalline but shows a pleasing blue aspect.

The Seventy-nine Mine is closed to collecting. A specimen miner from Globe works the Seventy-nine intermittently and the product of that labor is marketed through rock shops in Globe. The John Mediz shop in Globe can usually supply Seventy-nine specimens and can supply current information on the mine and its minerals.

SITE 6: *MAMMOTH/ST. ANTHONY MINE*

The Mammoth/St. Anthony Mine, at times called The Tiger, was one of the premier specimen mines in the Southwest, and maybe the world. The complex ore of the three mines (Mammoth, Collins, and Mohawk) that formed the Mammoth/St. Anthony enjoyed six stages of mineralization. The showiest specimens (wulfenite, vanadinite, and dioptase) were made during the fifth and sixth stages.

Mining began on the property during 1879. Gold was the only ore. More than 150,000 ounces of the yellow metal were recovered by 1901 (at a yield of three million pre-inflation dollars), when the Mammoth vein (the primary workings at the time) caved from the surface to the 750-foot level. A World War I demand for molybdenum and vanadium caused renewed interest, and

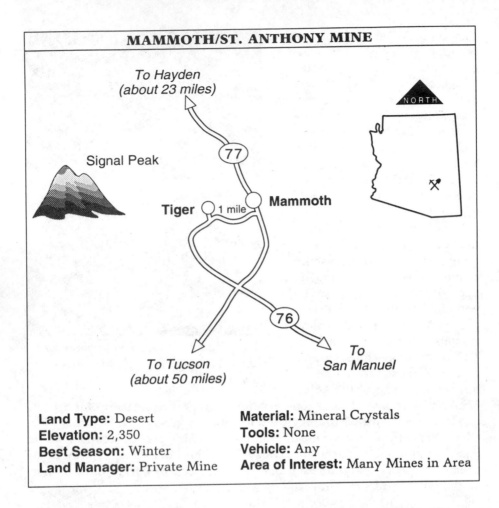

MAMMOTH/ST. ANTHONY MINE

To Hayden
(about 23 miles)

Signal Peak

77

Tiger ○ 1 mile Mammoth

NORTH

76

To Tucson
(about 50 miles)

To
San Manuel

Land Type: Desert
Elevation: 2,350
Best Season: Winter
Land Manager: Private Mine

Material: Mineral Crystals
Tools: None
Vehicle: Any
Area of Interest: Many Mines in Area

the property was worked from 1915 until 1919 for those metals. An increase in the price of gold in 1933 caused the property to be reopened, and the oxidized areas of the veins were worked for gold, vanadium, and molybdenum until about 1943. A demand for base metals caused the company to extend the workings to the sulphide ore bodies below the 650-foot level of the Collins Vein. Mineral collectors worldwide, if they had known the future, would have stood and cheered.

The best specimens produced came out of the sulphide ore body of the Collins Shaft—handsome wulfenite crystals in bold reds, oranges, and yellows, at times perched on a velvet carpet of a bright green dioptase; cerussite of cunningly intricate form; gobs of blood-red vanadinite coating country rock to form specimens as large as road apples; flat tabs of wulfenite coated with grassy green malachite; and too many more combinations to mention. Nearly every important museum in the world has specimens of the Tiger booty. Many local collectors added Tiger specimens to their personal collections.

The complex ore could not be worked at the mine. Gold ore was transported to the town of Mammoth, on the San Pedro River, by buckets suspended from a cable. The buckets carried water from the San Pedro on the return trip.

The underground workings have caved and are not accessible. "No trespassing" signs are posted at the dump. Once or twice a year local gem and mineral clubs are allowed to pick the dumps as a field trip. Collectors who live in the greater Tucson area occasionally release Tiger specimens. The annual Tucson show might be a possible source.

SITE 7: *BISBEE MINE*

Jack Dunn was scouting for water for the Army when he came upon the piece of cerussite. Dunn knew enough about minerals to get excited. He knew that cerussite, a carbonate of lead, sometimes carried significant silver values. Dunn reported the find to George Warren and loaned him money to buy equipment, a process called grubstaking. Warren, a man of devious character, took in partners and staked a number of claims, leaving Dunn out in the cold (or, as is most likely, out in the heat). One of those claims would later become the property called the Copper Queen Mine.

George Warren would have become a millionaire if his nature had allowed. Instead, under the influence of a bolt or two of white lightning, he bet his interest in the claims on a horse race. Warren was convinced he could outrun a horse over a short course. The horse won easily and the property that was to become the major copper producer in Arizona (you might just as well say the whole durn world), a mine that was destined to yield up a series of spectacular crystallizations of minerals too many to mention, passed to new hands.

Discovery occurred during 1877. Three years later, a smelter was completed and serious mining commenced. The mining camp within the Mule Mountains was a hell on earth. Open sewage ran in the street and the air was fouled by a cloud of sulfur dioxide smoke emitted by the smelter. The miners stayed drunk as much as possible. Shootings were commonplace.

The meager stringer of copper-influenced lead blossomed into a twenty percent copper (carbonates) ore body a few feet down. By 1900 Bisbee was giving up three million pounds of copper each month. Calcites within the ore caused beautiful crystallizations of azurite and malachite to form. There were times when the vein opened up within natural limestone caverns and the walls of those underground caves would be coated with the greens and blues of the copper carbonates. Miners would hire a band, take their wives and girlfriends underground, and hold a dance. The company, it has been reported, held at least one board of directors meeting within such a crystal-coated cavern.

Decreasing ore value, increasing labor costs, and a low copper price

This petite specimen of selenite came from a small pocket within the Cole Shaft of the Copper Queen Mine.

caused the pit and underground workings at the Copper Queen to stop in 1975.

When Phelps Dodge closed the mines, the economy of Bisbee staggered. Miners moved out and the real estate market was flooded with property. Artists, writers, and others of a Bohemian persuasion moved in. The area evolved into a tourist attraction.

Specimens of Bisbee minerals can be seen at nearly every mineral museum in southern Arizona and within many museums worldwide. Important private collections contain the best of Bisbee azurite, malachite, cuprite, selenite, calcite, and native copper. A complete list of the rare and semi-rare coppers recovered here would fill a page.

Bisbee holds many attractions even now, including fascinating examples of turn-of-the-century architecture. The Copper Queen Hotel offers a look at a suite of Bisbee minerals. Retired miners conduct hour-long underground tours. An hour-and-a-half bus ride offers a close look at the inactive Lavender Pit. The arts and crafts community offers all sorts of interesting gee-gaws, some in the form of jewelry that contains examples of the extra-fine blue and red turquoise that came from parts of the ore body. **Public collecting is not allowed.** For full information, contact the Greater Bisbee Chamber of Commerce, 78 Main Street, P.O. Drawer BA, Bisbee, AZ 85603; phone (602) 432-2141. To reserve space on the Copper Queen Mine tour, call (602) 432-2071.

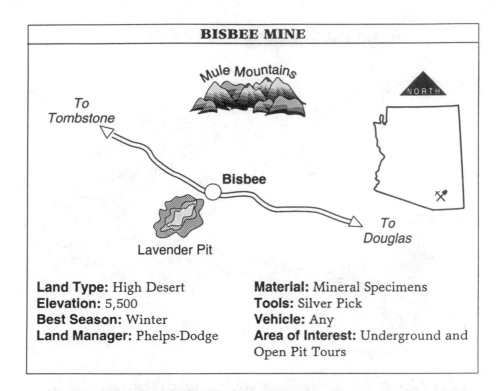

BISBEE MINE

Mule Mountains

To Tombstone

NORTH

Bisbee

Lavender Pit

To Douglas

Land Type: High Desert
Elevation: 5,500
Best Season: Winter
Land Manager: Phelps-Dodge

Material: Mineral Specimens
Tools: Silver Pick
Vehicle: Any
Area of Interest: Underground and Open Pit Tours

SITE 8: *DUQUESNE/WASHINGTON CAMP MINES*

The mining districts of Duquesne (say Doo-cain) and Washington Camp are nearly contiguous, being separated by less than a mile. The two districts, almost always, are called **Washington Camp**. During the late 1880s, eighty claims covered more than 1,600 acres of mining ground within the two districts. Lead from area mines, it has been said, supplied bullets for Confederate guns during the Civil War. Washington Camp mines have yielded up monstrously fine crystallizations of quartz. Some of those crystal groups showed the quartz crystallizing in the Jap Twin habit. More than a few incorporated fine calcite, the calcite and the quartz cooperating to produce mineral specimens of unusual beauty and interest.

The Holland Mine has relinquished Jap Twin crystals with "ears" more than a foot long. The Holland dumps can be generous to this day.

The primary mine within the Duquesne District was—and is—the Duquesne. This mine began production during 1899 and returned about four million dollars worth of ore during the next twenty-five years.

The Pride of the West was an important mine within the Washington Camp District. The Pride was located in 1880, primarily as a copper property. The highly complex ore carried important secondary values in lead, zinc, gold, and silver. The Washington Camp District, supported mainly by the

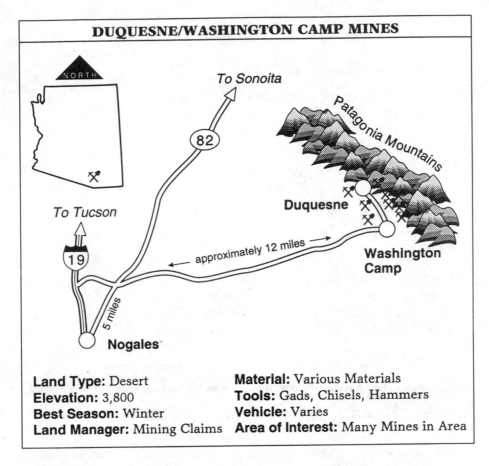

DUQUESNE/WASHINGTON CAMP MINES

NORTH

To Sonoita

82

To Tucson

19

Duquesne

Patagonia Mountains

Washington Camp

approximately 12 miles

5 miles

Nogales

Land Type: Desert
Elevation: 3,800
Best Season: Winter
Land Manager: Mining Claims

Material: Various Materials
Tools: Gads, Chisels, Hammers
Vehicle: Varies
Area of Interest: Many Mines in Area

Pride of the West mine, had a population of more than 1,000 in 1901. One-and-a-half million pre-inflation dollars were earned between 1899 and 1907.

Other mines, not within either the Duquesne or Washington Camp districts but within the region, gave up superb mineral specimens. One such was the Flux Mine, sometimes called the Trench-Flux because the two were contiguous and were often worked as a single property. Both mines were located in 1850. Each worked a separate ore body.

The Flux is famous among mineral collectors because of the particularly fine specimens of jackstraw cerussite found here—the jumble of snow-white "straws" perched on a hard limonite base.

Thousands of mines and prospects pockmark this area of Arizona. The dumps of many offer exciting collecting opportunities. Most of the properties within the region date to the 1860s. Hundreds and maybe thousands of mineral hounds have visited some of the dumps. Even so, the dumps offer booty to those willing to work. A small prospect located a bit north of the town of Patagonia, for example, recently gave up superb crystals of the lead vanadate called vanadinite. Inch-long crystals of a red-brown vanadinite graced plates of rock.

Not all "abandoned" mines are truly abandoned. Many are periodically worked. Some are no longer active but are dangerous. Others are posted with no trespass signs. Each collector has a responsibility to ascertain status and safety before attempting to collect.

Washington Camp quartz was some of the best in the world.

SITE 9: *COPPER AND MINERALS AT AJO*

The New Cornelia Pit at Ajo is idle. Diminishing ore values, increased production costs, and a low copper value caused the historic mine to cease production during the 1980s. A skeleton crew remains to protect the property and to maintain the equipment.

The Ajo Pit, as it is commonly called, produced a generous assortment of minerals and cuttables when active. Some say that the best specimens of native copper found anywhere in the world came from Ajo. Often the crystals of copper were found encased in a massive calcite. The protecting calcite was etched away to expose the undamaged crystals of copper.

Other copper-influenced crystals were recovered. The hairy cuprite called chalcotrichite, the miners "plush copper," was found in the typical rich reds. One massive pocket yielded up deep blue azurite crystals, some partially altered to malachite. There have been others, too many to mention.

A ledge of the overburden yielded up thousands of pounds of the cuttable shattuckite. Other parts of the pit produced chrysocolla with copper inclusions, chrysocolla with tenorite (black) inclusions, and half a handful of other rare rough.

A meager supply of the exotic material continues to be available. Much of

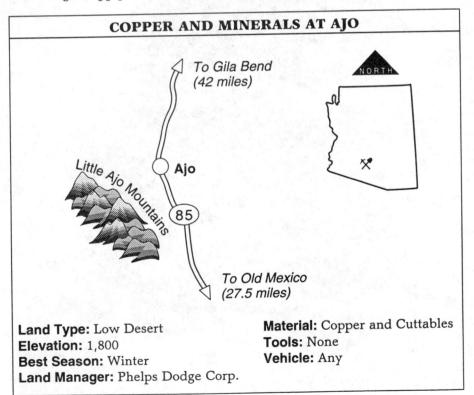

COPPER AND MINERALS AT AJO

To Gila Bend (42 miles)

NORTH

Little Ajo Mountains

Ajo

85

To Old Mexico (27.5 miles)

Land Type: Low Desert
Elevation: 1,800
Best Season: Winter
Land Manager: Phelps Dodge Corp.

Material: Copper and Cuttables
Tools: None
Vehicle: Any

it likely comes from the personal collections or hoardings of the former miners. It is probable that other parts may come from freshly mined material, perhaps mined and marketed by the maintenance crew or by former employees who have access to the pit.

The hills that surround the town of Ajo are pockmarked with prospects and idle mines. The dumps of those workings are likely to contain specimens of interest to the lapidary and to the mineral collector. A collector who visits here during the mild winter months, one who has a vehicle equipped for desert travel, might find cuttables and collectables of unusual quality.

Silver pick collecting at Ajo will be somewhat productive. Attend a meeting of the rockhound club to become acquainted with locals. Bring along quality material for trading. You will almost surely meet some mighty fine folks. If you are extra lucky you will leave the desert town of Ajo (which is also the name for a wild garlic) with a few quality specimens.

SITE 10: *RARE COPPERS AT GRANDVIEW*

The Grandview Mine is located about two-thirds of the way between the south rim of the Grand Canyon and the Colorado River. A tortuous series of switchbacks provides access. The carcass of the mine is located within the Grand Canyon National Park, where **no collecting is permitted.**

The Grandview enjoyed a short life as a copper producer. High-grade ore

Ore from the Grandview Mine was hauled to the rim of the Grand Canyon on burro back.

was loaded upon the back of mules to make the arduous trip to the top. A structure there, the Grandview Hotel, provided shelter for the workers.

This remote property was located in 1890 (before Grand Canyon National Park was established). Ore from the mine was displayed at the Columbia Exposition in Chicago during 1895 and was awarded first prize for assaying out at over seventy percent pure copper. The Grandview ore was rich in copper sulfates, such as the rare cyanotrichite, brochantite, and chalcoalumette. The common copper carbonates were also present (azurite and malachite). Many other rare and semi-rare crystallizations have been recovered, many as beautiful, velvety aggregates.

William Randolph Hearst purchased the below-rim and on-rim property in 1913. Fear that he would commercialize it may have hurried protective legislation. Grand Canyon National Park was established in 1916 and mining, and collecting, ceased.

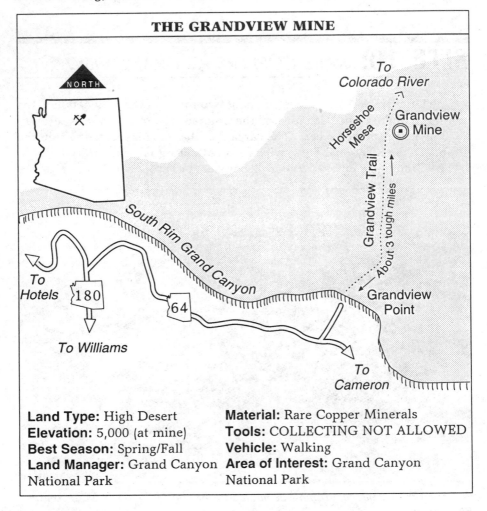

THE GRANDVIEW MINE

NORTH

To Colorado River

Grandview Mine

Horseshoe Mesa

Grandview Trail

About 3 tough miles

South Rim Grand Canyon

To Hotels 180

64

To Williams

Grandview Point

To Cameron

Land Type: High Desert
Elevation: 5,000 (at mine)
Best Season: Spring/Fall
Land Manager: Grand Canyon National Park

Material: Rare Copper Minerals
Tools: COLLECTING NOT ALLOWED
Vehicle: Walking
Area of Interest: Grand Canyon National Park

SITE 11: *RED CLOUD WULFENITE*

The Red Cloud Mine is world famous as a quality wulfenite producer. The crystals found here are mainly a saturated red. The stout, tabular crystals are splendent and sometimes occur as single crystals of uncommon beauty. Early operators worked the Red Cloud Mine as a silver producer prior to 1881. They removed more than $330,000 worth of silver from the croppings. Currently the mine consists of a somewhat steep incline shaft that descends to groundwater level (500 feet).

The shaft is regularly interrupted by stopes and drifts. Many of these "glory holes" have been backfilled, an economical way of disposing of gangue from lower workings. Many of the stopes were accessible when the author collected there during the mid-1960s.

The vein is chiefly limonite, hematite, quartz, fluorite, and calcite. Considerable gouge is present. The wulfenite (and at times cerussite) occurs in small to mid-size pockets, much of it in the limonite.

Unlike most wulfenite producers, the Red Cloud Mine offers up a wulfenite-bearing stringer at the surface. Like most other properties in the Silver District, the Red Cloud sits on patented property. **Underground collecting is never allowed, but surface collecting is sometimes allowed.** Gamblers may wish to sacrifice the day needed to travel the rough road to the mine, hoping they will be allowed to collect.

Collecting underground at the Red Cloud was dangerous when

Above: *The late Lou Boettcher ties off a timber for the trip into the Red Cloud Mine. Vandals destroyed the buildings in the background.* **Left:** *Red Cloud Wulfenite shows a splendent red surface.*

the author visited there and is more dangerous today. Shafts and stopes are in disrepair. The ground is unstable. Many of the stopes, particularly at the lower levels, hold bad air. Do not bet your life against the chance of obtaining a mineral specimen. **Do not attempt to collect underground at the Red Cloud or at any other inactive mine.**

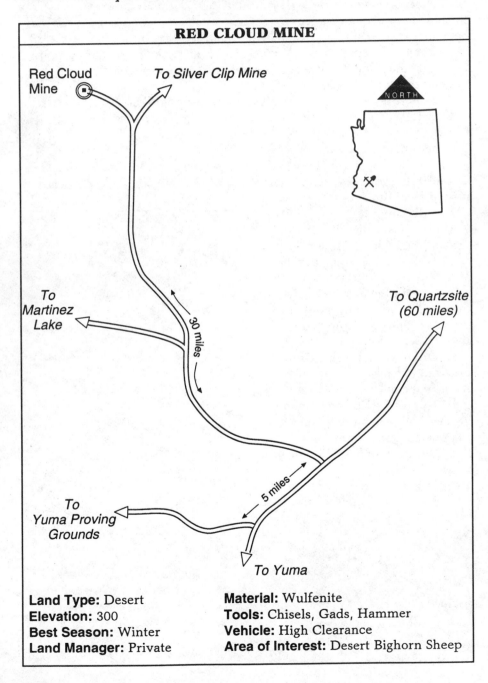

RED CLOUD MINE

Red Cloud Mine

To Silver Clip Mine

NORTH

To Martinez Lake

30 miles

To Quartzsite (60 miles)

To Yuma Proving Grounds

5 miles

To Yuma

Land Type: Desert
Elevation: 300
Best Season: Winter
Land Manager: Private

Material: Wulfenite
Tools: Chisels, Gads, Hammer
Vehicle: High Clearance
Area of Interest: Desert Bighorn Sheep

The dumps of other mines within the Silver District may yield up interesting crystallizations, particularly to the micromounter. The Black Rock Mine and the Papago Mine (south of the Red Cloud), and the Padre, Princess, and Silver Clip mines (to the north of the Red Cloud) have produced crystallizations.

The road that leads to the Silver District is primitive and long, about thirty miles. Much of it is slow going. A pickup truck is needed, and a pickup truck equipped with four-wheel drive and a winch is best. Avoid the area between May 15 and October 1. It is too hot for comfort, too hot for collecting, and too hot for safety.

SITE 12: *AMETHYST AT FOUR PEAKS*

The amethyst located within a saddle of the Four Peaks Mountain Range has been known and worked for centuries. Spanish explorers who passed through the area during the 1500s likely paused to collect specimens. It has been said that a portion of the royal purple amethyst found in the crown jewels of Spain came from the Four Peaks deposit.

The Four Peaks amethyst occurs in soft manganese clay. Most of the crystals occur as singles and as terminations only. The size of the crystals can be impressive. Several in the author's collection exceed the size of John Wayne's fist.

The exterior aspect of the crystals can vary. Many show a dark, dull finish. Others show a secondary growth of glass-clear quartz over the amethyst.

The color within these large crystals is mostly in bands or zones within the quartz. At times, color concentrates in the point of the termination. In either case, the stone must be carefully oriented before faceting.

As is the case with most gemstone deposits, the Four Peaks deposit holds amethyst that varies in color and quality. The best material easily attains the best grade of amethyst, that is, Siberian. The deep purple of the gem changes as the light source changes—a rich purple red under tungsten light and blue violet under fluorescent light. Sunlight causes the gem to flash with a bold red. Some specimens of Four Peaks amethyst can be greened by heat treating to produce a product called prasiolite.

The amethyst mine at Four Peaks is on a patented mining claim. A caretaker lives on site to protect the property. **Collecting is not permitted**. There is a lot of unpatented land in the area, however—public land that is a part of the Tonto National Forest. Other amethyst deposits likely occur within the craggy peaks of the range. Half a handful of collectors have braved the steep terrain (and the snakes) to return with an amethyst crystal that differs considerably from that found at the Four Peaks Mine. The off-mine crystals show both termination and prism. Crystals from the mine are most often terminations only. The off-mine crystals, according to reports, were found within seams of quartz that cut the mountain range on the Tonto Basin (east) side of the range.

Access to the mine is difficult. Four-wheel drive vehicles can negotiate a primitive forest service road (El Oso, The Bear) that leaves Arizona 188 close to the Tonto Arm of Roosevelt Lake. At road's end a well-maintained trail leads to the mine. Hikers in good physical condition will find that the journey to the mine area will take about three hours.

Again, a caution. Do not make the tough drive and the tough hike to the mine hoping to collect. You will not be allowed to do so.

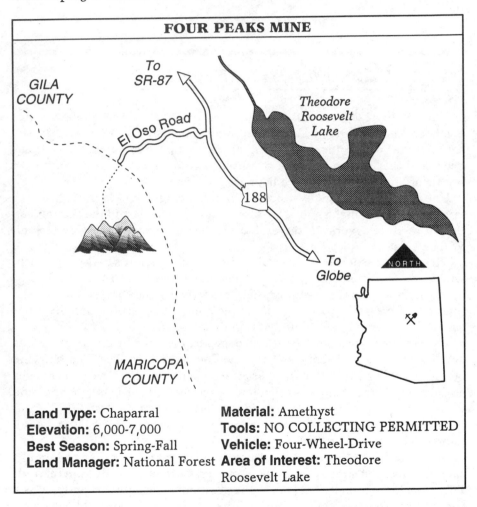

FOUR PEAKS MINE

Land Type: Chaparral
Elevation: 6,000-7,000
Best Season: Spring-Fall
Land Manager: National Forest

Material: Amethyst
Tools: NO COLLECTING PERMITTED
Vehicle: Four-Wheel-Drive
Area of Interest: Theodore Roosevelt Lake

SITE 13: *COURTLAND-GLEESON AREA MINES*

Many mines and prospects are scattered among this mostly contiguous area. Courtland may be best known because of the turquoise found here. Evidence shows that prehistoric Native Americans worked surface outcrops of turquoise. More modern Native Americans, the Apaches, fought to protect their area with fierce determination; thus, the area developed slowly.

Uncommonly rich surface stringers caused exploration to begin in earnest in about 1890. The rich outcrops brought many major mining companies flocking to the area that promised to be a second Bisbee. The surface indicators, alas, deceived. A half-mile square of copper rich rocks contained about all of the ore to be found here. Mines such as the Mary and the Gemania, rich at the surface, pinched out to barren rock at the 300-foot level.

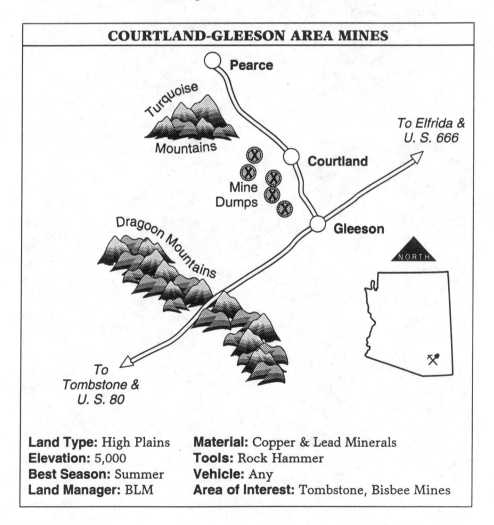

COURTLAND-GLEESON AREA MINES

Pearce

Turquoise Mountains

Mine Dumps

Courtland

To Elfrida & U. S. 666

Dragoon Mountains

Gleeson

NORTH

To Tombstone & U. S. 80

Land Type: High Plains
Elevation: 5,000
Best Season: Summer
Land Manager: BLM

Material: Copper & Lead Minerals
Tools: Rock Hammer
Vehicle: Any
Area of Interest: Tombstone, Bisbee Mines

Even though several of the mines yielded up a significant dollar value of ore, few did so at a profit to the owner.

The minerals found within the oxidized zone of that rich half-mile, however, were a diverse lot. Many were spectacular examples of copper and lead crystallizations.

Turquoise can be found on the dumps of mines and prospects located on the west side of Turquoise Ridge. Both the Gleeson and the Defiance mines have produced wulfenite specimens of great beauty. The best of the wulfenite showed a butterscotch aspect and crystals more than one inch wide. Another area of the mine offers an exciting yellow crystal that is as thin as paper and as clear as glass. These two mines offer smithsonite, aurichalcite, and rosasite.

The Courtland-Gleeson District, at one time called the Turquoise District, occupies an area about four miles long by two miles wide. Its principle features are a pair of ridges, Turquoise Ridge and Gleeson Ridge, separated by a narrow gulch. Principle mines within the district were The Tom Scott, The Silver Bill, The Mystery, The Defiance, and The 1907 (Last Chance).

The mine dumps of the many mines and prospects within the

Above right: *Wulfenite from the Defiance Mine came in butterscotch-colored crystals.* **Above:** *Cavities within the mines of the Courtland/Gleeson District contained a great number of calcite and quartz crystallizations.*

district offer an exciting diversity of minerals. Some have been mentioned. Others include pyrite and excellent bornite, called peacock copper because of the multicolor iridescence.

Just as with any private property, the collector has the responsibility to obtain permission to trespass when possible. Inquiry within the area will usually provide ownership information. Some dumps will be posted. Honor the owner's wishes. **Resist all temptation to trespass underground.** Most (maybe all) of the mines have been long inactive. The years and a lack of maintenance have caused the timbers to weaken with dry rot.

SITE 14: *ROWLEY MINE WULFENITE*

The Rowley is a bad mine, extremely dangerous. Part of the ore body consists of fractured barite, the kind that groans and gravels at the least excuse. Miners who worked the mine when it was most active, when the timbers were new and strong, worked with one eye on the ore and the other on the fastest way to the surface.

Having said that, the author should also point out that the Rowley has given up thousands of breathtakingly beautiful wulfenite/mimetite crystallizations. The orange-yellow wulfenite sometimes is decorated with orange-red balls of mimetite. This handsome cooperation is at times perched on a pleasant blue ore. The totality of the aspect must be seen to be appreciated.

Much of the Rowley wulfenite is hemimorphic (half form). A few crystals in the author's collection are fully formed (up to one inch), transparent, and coated with the mimetite balls.

The main access to the mine is a badly caved incline shaft that leads to water level (about 125 feet down). The ladder is in dangerous disrepair. A tunnel goes right and left past the end of the incline. The right-hand tunnel is closed and mostly inaccessible. The left-hand tunnel leads to a continuation of the shaft (flooded) and to a number of rooms. The rooms carry mostly the fractured and dangerous barite. Cavities within the barite carry the crystallizations.

The underground workings are closed to collectors. The workings were dangerous when the author collected there

This specimen from the Rowley Mine workings shows bright yellow wulfenite adorned with orange acicular mimetite.

twenty-five years ago and are more dangerous now. The Rowley dumps can be collected, however, and hard work will almost always be rewarded with micromount specimens, and on rare occasions, thumbnail-sized crystallizations. A miniature or a cabinet specimen shows once in a great while.

The best technique involves work with chisels, gads, and cracking hammers. Part of the dump gangue will show a thin seam of color. Using the chisel or gad to expose that vein sometimes will cause a crystal pocket to appear. The wulfenite crystals are thin and fragile. The shock of the hammer may cause them to fracture loose from the base. Sometimes not. If an undamaged crystal pocket is discovered, pack the rock carefully for the trip home. Final trimming should be done using a rock splitter powered by a hydraulic jack.

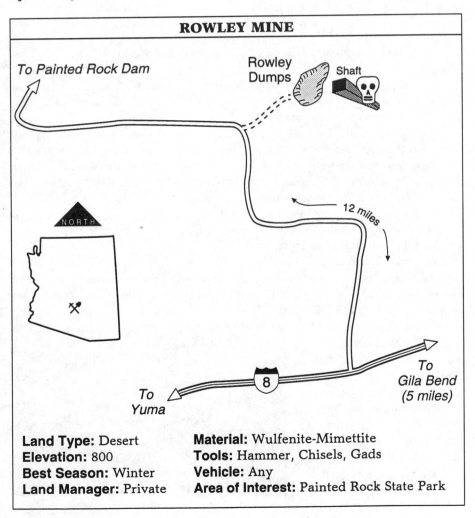

ROWLEY MINE

To Painted Rock Dam

Rowley Dumps

Shaft

NORTH

12 miles

To Yuma

8

To Gila Bend (5 miles)

Land Type: Desert
Elevation: 800
Best Season: Winter
Land Manager: Private

Material: Wulfenite-Mimettite
Tools: Hammer, Chisels, Gads
Vehicle: Any
Area of Interest: Painted Rock State Park

Old Mines are dangerous places—rotten timbers, crumbling rock, and toxic vapors just waiting for the next victim. Stay out and stay alive.

SITE 15: *SCENIC SANDSTONE*

Deposits of scenic sandstone have been found along the Arizona-Utah border near Fredonia. The rock is highly prized and commercial firms have filed claims on much of the available material. A busy shop located at the north end of Fredonia offers rough and slabbed material.

Much of the slabbed sandstone shows shades of tan and brown cooperating to form a series of rolling "hills." The Shinarump formation that carries the picture rock is a fine-grained sandstone deposited during the Triassic Period (about 150 million years ago). The Shinarump rests between the

Moenkopi and Chinle sandstone layers. Bulldozers are used to expose the Shinarump layer and pieces are hand-sorted. Diamond saws do the slabbing. Then the slabs are trimmed to form rectangles that are framed, serving as wall decor. Other slabs of the scenic sandstone are painted so that the applied image cunningly cooperates with the natural lines to form a whole.

A most attractive sort of sandstone is marketed by a rock supply firm in St. George, Utah. The material is extremely fine-grained sandstone showing a generally white aspect. A bold brown pattern intrudes to compose interesting scenics.

Do not use oil as a saw coolant when cutting this type of material. Water works best. Use a softer piece of sandstone to hand rub away the saw marks.

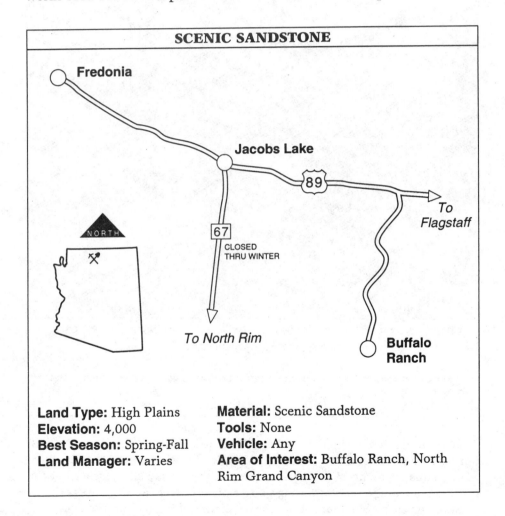

SCENIC SANDSTONE

Fredonia

Jacobs Lake

89

67

CLOSED
THRU WINTER

NORTH

To
Flagstaff

To North Rim

Buffalo
Ranch

Land Type: High Plains
Elevation: 4,000
Best Season: Spring-Fall
Land Manager: Varies

Material: Scenic Sandstone
Tools: None
Vehicle: Any
Area of Interest: Buffalo Ranch, North Rim Grand Canyon

SITE 16: *CALCITE AND CERUSSITE NEAR SUPAI*

The Havasupai tribal village lies in a side canyon that connects to Arizona's Grand Canyon. The remote village can be reached only by a nine-mile foot trail or by horseback. The trip, nearly all agree, is worth the effort. The small village is located in a most picturesque setting. Havasupai Creek flows through the village. Downstream a mile or two, the creek leaps from the first of a series of spectacular waterfalls. The last, Havasupai Falls, is breathtaking. The blue-green water drops more than a hundred feet into a pleasant pool. The high calcite content of the water has caused travertine dams to form through sections of the pool.

A side canyon that angles to the west of this pool, Carbonate Canyon, was the site of early-day mining. Hardy miners worked lead ore from the remote prospect. Mules carried the ore the many miles to Hilltop where it was trucked to smelters.

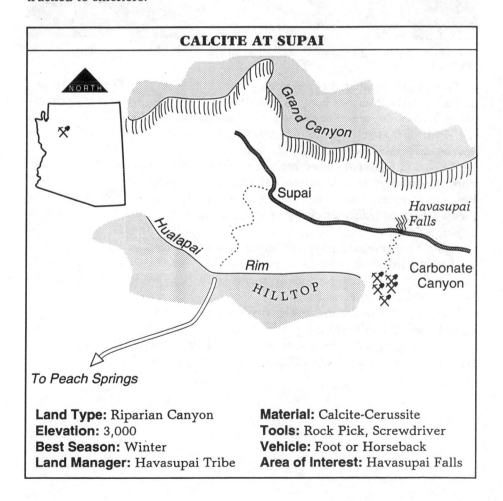

CALCITE AT SUPAI

NORTH

Grand Canyon

Supai

Havasupai Falls

Hualapai

Rim

HILLTOP

Carbonate Canyon

To Peach Springs

Land Type: Riparian Canyon
Elevation: 3,000
Best Season: Winter
Land Manager: Havasupai Tribe

Material: Calcite-Cerussite
Tools: Rock Pick, Screwdriver
Vehicle: Foot or Horseback
Area of Interest: Havasupai Falls

Havasupai Falls, with Carbonate Canyon to the left in the background.

The mine is located about a mile up Carbonate Canyon. The short tunnel contains the exposed ore body, where chunks of poorly crystallized cerussite can be found. These are limonite-covered and are mineralogically uninteresting. Within that same limonite gouge, however, are excellent crystals of yellow calcite. Some exhibit the fish-tail twins habit.

Rock and mineral collecting regulations are set by individual tribal councils and it is not known if collecting is currently permitted. Readers interested in a sightseeing/collecting trip to the Havasupai can receive current information by contacting the Havasupai Tribal Council, Supai, AZ 86435.

Again, the mine in Carbonate Canyon is remotely located. The fifteen-mile walk to the mine, or at best, the nine-mile horseback ride and the six-mile walk to the mine, can be physically taxing. Only those who are in top physical condition should attempt the trip.

Collecting at the Carbonate Canyon Mine requires a minimum of tools. A hand trowel is handy, as is a pair of large screwdrivers to use as prys. The crystals are dirty with limonite mud when collected. Wash them (perhaps in Havasupai Creek) and inspect them before the pack out.

SITE 17: *CREAMY ONYX NEAR KINGMAN*

The deposit of onyx found on a southeast slope of Stockton Hill yields up a product that is solid and banded. White and cream bands alternate to form an attractive gem rough.

The material is not onyx in the mineralogical definition, but is, instead, a calcareous limestone. Travertine would be a more appropriate name. The high calcite content makes the material semi-soft. Conventional lapidary treatment seldom provides acceptable results. Stockton Hill onyx is used mainly as a material for table tops and book ends.

The Mohave County Gemstoners (Kingman) have filed a mining claim on the deposit to prevent commercial exploitation. To reach the deposit, take the Stockton Hill Road as it exits Interstate 40 (Exit 51) and travel north for about ten miles. Watch for diggings to your left. A primitive two track leads from the paved road to the diggings.

Small cobbles of onyx can be collected from the dumps. Collectors who wish fresh material of a larger size must get it the old-fashioned way. They must work for it. Sledge hammers, gads, and chisels are required. These tools,

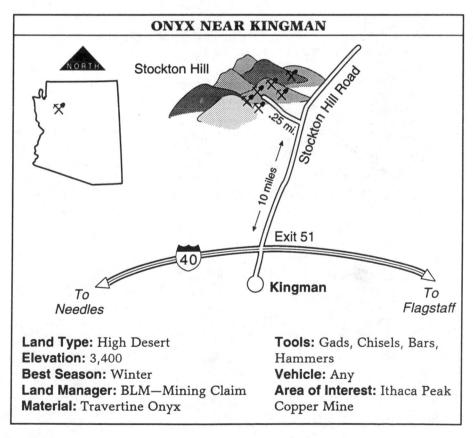

ONYX NEAR KINGMAN

Stockton Hill

NORTH

Stockton Hill Road

.25 mi.

10 miles

Exit 51

40

To Needles

Kingman

To Flagstaff

Land Type: High Desert
Elevation: 3,400
Best Season: Winter
Land Manager: BLM—Mining Claim
Material: Travertine Onyx

Tools: Gads, Chisels, Bars, Hammers
Vehicle: Any
Area of Interest: Ithaca Peak Copper Mine

hard work, perspiration, (and at times strong language), will cause the onyx seam to yield up its best material.

The Stockton Hill material is best worked on a wet sander. The semi-soft nature of the material will cause it to cut too rapidly on the grinder. Proceed through the grits using a well-worn 600 for the finish. Polish using tin or chrome oxide on leather. Even though some authorities advise adding a few crystals of oxalic acid to the oxide, and even though such a mixture might improve polish, it is not recommended. The dangerous nature of the oxalic acid offsets the small gain in sheen. A person who is patient can nearly equal the acid-induced polish using straight oxide.

Hobbyists who carve will find the Stockton Hill material a joy to work. Soft enough to be worked with most steel tools, the material is solid and fracture-free. Even though the deposit is under claim, the Kingman Club has allowed amateur collecting without fee. Local inquiry might be advisable to determine current status.

SITE 18: *FIRE AGATE AT BLACK MOUNTAINS*

Silversmith Doug McVicar of Kingman fashioned this fiery bola from agate collected along The Flats.

The detritus that has eroded from the eastern slope of the Black Mountain Range carries a considerable amount of chalcedony. Some of that chalcedony contains the sardonyx band that produces fire agate.

The chalcedony scattered along the flats and slopes of the eastern aspect of the Black Mountain Range is there as float. The material apparently eroded away from a deposit on the higher slopes of the Black Mountain Range.

Not a lot of fire agate is found at this location. A sharp-eyed collector might hunt for several hours and find only a few keepers. The pieces that do contain fire, however, contain the same attractive fire as that found in the fire agate from the fee area to the north— flashy gold, mostly, with occasional flashes of green. Red fire is sometimes found.

Hunting the area will be most productive during early fall. A summer of hard rains has scoured the flats and slopes to uncover a fresh supply of gemstone. Time your search early in the day, soon after sunup, or late in the afternoon. The low sun angle will make it easier to discover the chalcedony. Keep the sun behind you. Walk slowly. Pick up any rock showing the waxy white of the chalcedony to closely inspect. A thumbnail-sized piece of chalcedony, at times, will turn to a palm-sized piece of fire agate when the dirt has been kicked away.

Some of the chalcedony, even though it does not contain fire, can be used to cut attractive cabochons.

The Flats, as they are called locally, have been a steady producer of fire agate and chalcedony for many years. The nature of the deposit nearly ensures a continuing supply of material.

To reach the collecting area, take Interstate 40 west from Kingman to the McConnico exit. Travel west on the Oatman-Goldroad for about twenty miles. You will see the Black Mountain Range ahead. Turn to the left on any of the roads that lead along the base of the mountains.

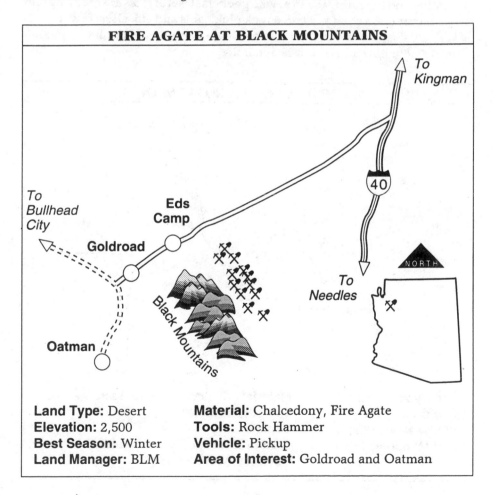

FIRE AGATE AT BLACK MOUNTAINS

Land Type: Desert
Elevation: 2,500
Best Season: Winter
Land Manager: BLM

Material: Chalcedony, Fire Agate
Tools: Rock Hammer
Vehicle: Pickup
Area of Interest: Goldroad and Oatman

SITE 19: *FIRE AGATE NEAR OATMAN*

The fire agate near Cool Springs, Arizona, within the Oatman-Goldroad Mining District, has been known and worked for more than fifty years. During the last half of those five decades, the deposit has been worked as a fee-collecting area. A modest fee permits the collector to enter the field to dig for fire agate. At publication, the property managers charge a $5 entry fee and make no extra charge for poundage.

A person who works hard and who has the proper tools can find fire agate at Cool Springs (later called Ed's Camp). Little surface material is available. The chalcedony occurs as boytroidal bubbles hidden away within vugs and cracks of a tough rhyolite. The owners do not remove overburden as is the case on some other fee collecting claims. Each collector must do the hard job of locating and liberating the fire agate pockets. Useful tools are cracking and sledge hammers, a stout pry bar, a rock pick, gads and chisels, screw drivers of various size, and a whisk broom to clean away dust. Gasoline-powered tools are not allowed. Neither is dynamite.

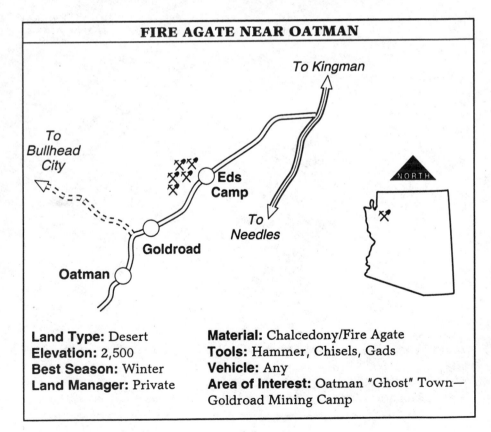

FIRE AGATE NEAR OATMAN

To Kingman

To Bullhead City

NORTH

Eds Camp

To Needles

Goldroad

Oatman

Land Type: Desert
Elevation: 2,500
Best Season: Winter
Land Manager: Private

Material: Chalcedony/Fire Agate
Tools: Hammer, Chisels, Gads
Vehicle: Any
Area of Interest: Oatman "Ghost" Town—Goldroad Mining Camp

Here are tips that might make the locating and digging a bit less hard. Look for above-ground features to learn a bit about underground features. A stingy stringer of above-ground chalcedony, for example, might open up underground into a decent crack or vug. Closely inspect desert vegetation, particularly those plants that appear to be growing on solid rock. Often, the plant is able to exist because the roots have discovered an underground crack or vug. Do not attempt to chip the chalcedony specimens in an effort to discover fire. Take the piece home, wash it carefully, and use the trim saw to remove the cap and expose the fire-bearing sardonyx.

The Cool Springs diggings are closed during the summer. Collecting is permitted during the cooler fall, winter, and spring. Loose-fitting, long-legged, and long-sleeved clothing is advised. Wear a wide-brimmed hat to keep most of the sun's rays from your face. Leather gloves are a necessity. Finally, if your trip is timed during fall or spring, watch for snakes.

Collecting information can be obtained by contacting Alma Snyder, Oatman Star Route, Box 905, Kingman, AZ 86401.

SITE 20: *RIVER ROCKS*

The ridges that lead from the Black Mountains to the Colorado River are composed of millions of tons of alluvium, carried here from a distant source. The boulders and cobbles that are the main part of the detritus are mostly uninteresting. But the waterworn rind of a few of the cobbles cover agate and jasper of unusual beauty. Much of the jewelry rock is agate or jasper of a brilliant red. Some cobbles may exhibit an interesting blue color. Others mix red and white (and sometimes blue) to form a patriotic rock that can be turned into bragging cabochons.

Some of the ridges have produced excellent specimens of petrified ironwood. The crust of the log and limb sections shows well-preserved bark (sometimes showing knotholes) and is a dirty white. The interior is a mixture of black and gray, usually with growth rings visible.

One area of interest is north and east of Katherines Landing. Travel upriver from the landing until you see a power transmission line crossing the road. Turn east (right) on this dirt road and explore the finger ridges that slope from the mountains.

As is often the case, the areas closest to the road are hardest hit. Collectors who are physically able should hike away from the roads a mile or two to discover virgin ground. You will not be able to collect a great quantity of material. The quality of the best material, however, makes the search worthwhile.

The nearby resort town of Bullhead City offers fine striped bass fishing along the Colorado River. Fish in the fifteen- to twenty- five-pound class are not uncommon. The Laughlin Casinos, on the Nevada side of the river, provide entertainment for those who have an itch to gamble. Nearly all of the casinos offer delicious buffet meals. Air conditioned rooms are available at rock-bottom rates.

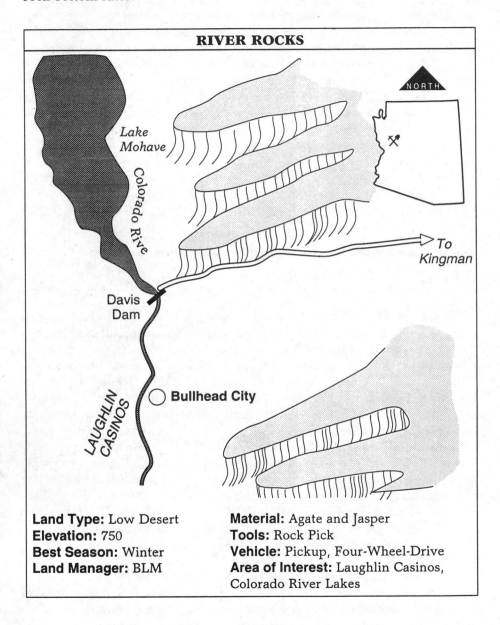

RIVER ROCKS

Land Type: Low Desert
Elevation: 750
Best Season: Winter
Land Manager: BLM

Material: Agate and Jasper
Tools: Rock Pick
Vehicle: Pickup, Four-Wheel-Drive
Area of Interest: Laughlin Casinos, Colorado River Lakes

SITE 21: *FLAGSTONE NEAR ASH FORK*

Flagstone, more properly called sandstone, is not a gem rough in the true sense of the term. Flagstone is essentially sand that has been compacted to form sedimentary layers of interesting rock. The material is mostly used as a building material and often appears as interior and exterior wall facings and as fireplace facings. The material has an eye-pleasing granular texture.

Some lapidaries have discovered a hobby application for flagstone. Thin slabs are pleasingly shaped to serve as a background for pictographic drawings. Metal and gemstone cutouts are attached to the flagstone using epoxy or a hot glue gun. The resulting color and textural contrast can be handsome.

The low hills to the north of the town of Ash Fork hold a plentitude of active and inactive flagstone quarries. Small slabs, too small for commercial use, abound. Many are right-sized for rockhound applications. As you collect, stay alert for slabs that show evidence of fossil inclusions and watch for slabs that have been stained by mineral inclusion. Such "scenic sandstone" can be particularly effective as the background for a painting.

To reach the quarries, take Forest Road 142 north from Ash Fork. Drive two miles to the junction of Forest Road 39 and turn right. About four miles later, you will see a cluster of quarries in the area of Antolini Hill.

A ten-square-mile area is pocked with the quarries. Stop at the Kaibab National Forest Ranger Station in the town of Williams to purchase a Kaibab forest map. You will find it immensely helpful, as the mines are marked with

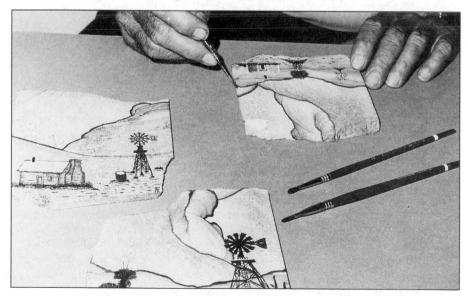

Foy Partain of Farmington, New Mexico, incorporates sandstone patterns into his paintings.

the crossed-pick symbol. Many, maybe even most, of the forest roads are somewhat primitive and are only occasionally maintained. Many are too primitive for a passenger car. Pickups are better and pickups equipped with four-wheel drive are best.

Some rockhounds do not saw the flagstone. It has natural cleavage planes that permit separation along the bedding plane. Pliers are then used to "nibble" the piece to shape.

If you must use the saw, do not use oil as the lubricant. Oil will permeate the sandstone and is apt to create a messy cleanup chore. After draining the oil, use warm soapy water to scrub away the residual oil and use a new batch of warm soapy water as a lubricant. If possible, saw other soft or porous material using the water as a coolant. Drain out the water when the job is done and return the oil. Leaving the water in the tank will almost surely cause the blade to rust.

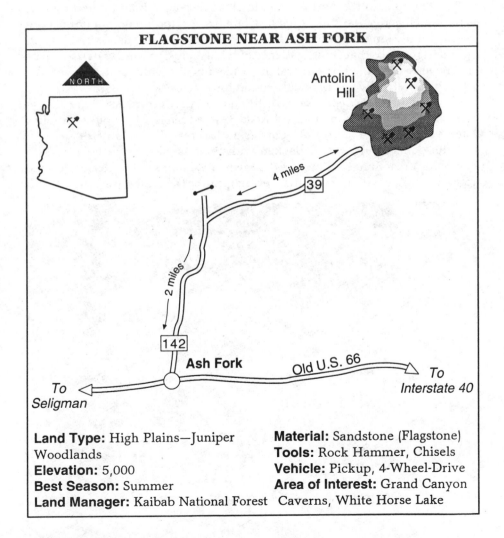

FLAGSTONE NEAR ASH FORK

Land Type: High Plains—Juniper Woodlands
Elevation: 5,000
Best Season: Summer
Land Manager: Kaibab National Forest

Material: Sandstone (Flagstone)
Tools: Rock Hammer, Chisels
Vehicle: Pickup, 4-Wheel-Drive
Area of Interest: Grand Canyon Caverns, White Horse Lake

SITE 22: *PETRIFIED WOOD NEAR JOSEPH CITY*

Specimen quality wood can be found within the low hills north of Interstate 40 between Joseph City and Holbrook. Some of the log sections are multi-ton monsters. Wood chips sometimes cover a hillside. The exterior of this easily identifiable wood is a dull tan or gray. The interior is much the same, showing an unremarkable aspect.

A diligent search may turn up an occasional piece of wood that is colorful and silicified. Agate, although scarce, will sometimes be found. A better quality wood has been found north of Joseph City near the south boundary of the Navajo Indian Reservation. A number of interesting washes cut through the Chinle Formation to expose the buried treasure. The wood found here is sometimes midnight black interrupted by zigzag lines of white.

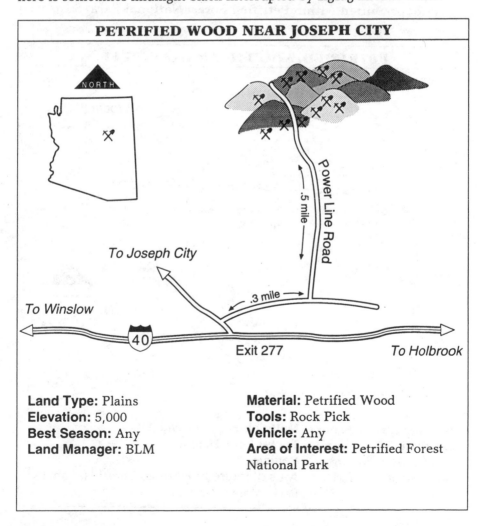

PETRIFIED WOOD NEAR JOSEPH CITY

To Joseph City

Power Line Road

.5 mile

.3 mile

To Winslow

40

Exit 277

To Holbrook

Land Type: Plains
Elevation: 5,000
Best Season: Any
Land Manager: BLM

Material: Petrified Wood
Tools: Rock Pick
Vehicle: Any
Area of Interest: Petrified Forest National Park

Some collectors have reported the discovery of the somewhat rare woodworthia here. The entire area from Joseph City north to the national park boundary (a distance of about forty miles) consists of the wood bearing Chinle. Much of the area is under-explored because of a scarcity of roads and the primitive nature of the few existing roads here. Much of the land is a part of vast cattle ranches and is closed to public entry.

SITE 23: *PETRIFIED WOOD NEAR WOODRUFF*

The northern half of Arizona, with one notable exception, holds little to interest the rock and mineral collector. That exception is the Petrified Forest National Park and the wood-bearing lands that surround the park. **Collecting is not permitted within Petrified Forest National Park.** Some who

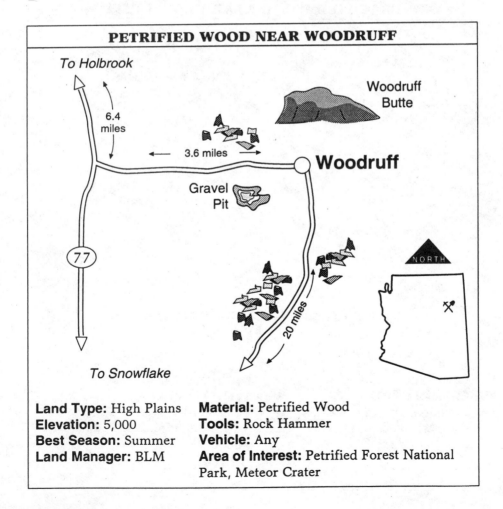

PETRIFIED WOOD NEAR WOODRUFF

To Holbrook

6.4 miles

3.6 miles

77

To Snowflake

Woodruff Butte

Woodruff

Gravel Pit

20 miles

NORTH

Land Type: High Plains
Elevation: 5,000
Best Season: Summer
Land Manager: BLM

Material: Petrified Wood
Tools: Rock Hammer
Vehicle: Any
Area of Interest: Petrified Forest National Park, Meteor Crater

own land near the park permit petrified wood collecting but charge a fee for the wood taken. (See "Petrified Wood on Dobell Ranch.") Some of the petrified wood-bearing ranchland has historically not permitted wood collecting, although there is a quantity of fine quality wood on much of it. There are areas, some located on private land and some on public land, that are accessible to the collector. The low hills to the west of Woodruff and the Silver Creek drainage to the south of this small community offer such a collecting opportunity. The public and private lands here offer petrified wood in small and semi-small pieces. Part of the material consists of fracture fragments fit only for the tumbler. The larger pieces of wood, some to fist size, hold cabbing possibilities. Much of the wood found is hard and colorful, with reds and yellows being somewhat common.

The wood occurs over many square miles of ranchland. Drive south from Holbrook on Arizona 77 for about 6.5 miles until you see the Woodruff turnoff to your left. Both sides of the road to the town of Woodruff (about 3.5 miles) hold petrified wood. An abandoned sand and gravel pit about a mile west of Woodruff has been a steady producer of wood—some pieces weighing up to twenty pounds. The area that surrounds the pit, although heavily hit by collectors, continues to produce.

Turn right (south) at Woodruff on the road that parallels Silver Creek to find further collecting opportunity. The land on both sides of this well-maintained dirt road will offer wood for a distance of about twenty miles, or, nearly to the town of Snowflake. Wood colors tend to reds, yellows, and whites.

The author collected in this area a few years back and noticed a fist-sized chunk of wood peeking from the soil. A casual kick did not dislodge or even budge the chunk. Digging with the rock pick proved ineffective. A trip to the truck for pick and shovel, and an hour or so of hard work, uncovered a 125-pound chunk of petrified rainbow. The reds, yellows, and purples within were breathtakingly beautiful. And unlike much of the surface wood found here, the log section was essentially unfractured.

Petrified wood from the Woodruff area should be washed in warm soapy water to remove the dirt and grime. After drying, inspect the wood to discover the degree of fracturing. Badly fractured material should be set aside as fodder for the tumbler, or to be retained as specimen material.

Make a second examination just before you place the material to the saw. Orient the cut to take best advantage of color, pattern, and lack of fracturing.

Slabbed wood should also be inspected for fractures. Do your looking while the slab is dry and make the examination under adequate illumination (sunlight is great). Some rockers find it helpful to use a magnifier such as an Opti-Visor. They use a permanent marker such as a Quickie to trace over external and internal fracture lines. The tracings can be helpful when it comes time to template out a cabochon.

Work the wood wet through the 320 grit grinder. Sand wet through the 600 grit cloth. Polish on rough or smooth leather using tin or cerium oxide. For a super polish, finish off with red rouge on muslin.

SITE 24: *PETRIFIED WOOD ON DOBELL RANCH*

The old Dobell Ranch is a combination of private and leased land that borders part of the west boundary to Petrified Forest National Park. The lands contain a generous allotment of petrified wood, much similar in color and quality to the wood found across the national park fence. Commercial and casual collecting has caused much of the surface material to disappear. Much of the surface material that remains is of poor quality.

Petrified wood of fine quality remains underground. The continuing process of erosion causes buried wood to be exposed. A casual collector always has the opportunity to discover some of this recently exposed material.

The lease holder is involved in an ongoing search for buried logs. He employs a ditch witch (a trenching machine) to locate multi-ton logs that may be buried a couple-dozen feet underground. When a log is located, a backhoe moves in to excavate. Exposed log sections are lifted to a flatbed truck and are sold to foreign sources. This commercial activity benefits those who visit here to casually collect. The operation exposes fresh wood—a lot of it—for collector examination.

The Dobell Ranch was managed by the Patton family for many years. For much of that time, the family permitted casual collecting on a fee basis. Rockhounds from all parts of the country visited to collect and pay the modest poundage fee.

The lessees at the Dobell Ranch excavate huge sections of petrified logs for export. Smaller pieces are made available to the collector.

The property changed hands in 1990, and collecting rules have been changed. Jim Gray, a principal of K&G Investments, states that his company will no longer allow unescorted collecting. Too often, he says, a collector would use his or her hammer to beat away at valuable pieces of wood in an attempt to fracture off a pound or two. Often the piece that was left was badly fractured and not saleable.

The new rules permit casual collecting. A K&G Investments employee will accompany the collector to the field. A $250 collecting minimum is in effect. The fee charged for the wood collected will be between $.70 and $1.00 per pound, according to Gray. Groups or individuals who desire to collect at the Dobell Ranch are advised to make prior arrangements through K&G Investments, P.O. Box 850, Holbrook, AZ 80025; phone (602) 524-3500.

The Dobell Ranch wood is true rainbow wood, much of it carrying strong reds, yellows, blacks, and whites. Some pieces show the alternating yellow and purple banding locally called candy-striping. Other specimens might show the red and black of picture wood. Collectors are advised to bring picks, shovels, and pry bars. Leather gloves and safety glasses will be helpful.

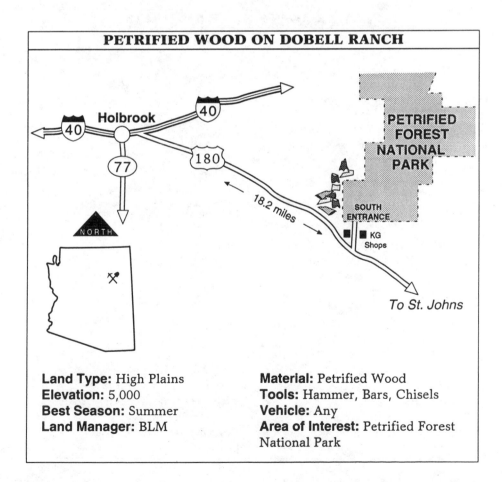

PETRIFIED WOOD ON DOBELL RANCH

Holbrook — 40 — 77 — 180 — 18.2 miles — To St. Johns

PETRIFIED FOREST NATIONAL PARK

SOUTH ENTRANCE

KG Shops

NORTH

Land Type: High Plains
Elevation: 5,000
Best Season: Summer
Land Manager: BLM

Material: Petrified Wood
Tools: Hammer, Bars, Chisels
Vehicle: Any
Area of Interest: Petrified Forest National Park

SITE 25: *FLOWER AGATE NEAR ST. JOHNS*

The agate found north of St. Johns occurs in a massive seam that seems localized to one small area. The material is a confused conglomeration of reds, whites, blacks, and rarely, yellow. The most attractive cabochons are cut from material that contains a lot of white with red, black, and yellow spotting the white infrequently. Even though it will accept a fine polish, much of the material is so dark and dense, it does not show the pattern and the color.

The agate deposit is on land that has been leased by Reginald Richey of St. Johns. A locked gate six miles west of the deposit denies entry. Richey has operated the area as a fee-collecting site in the past and continues to do on an intermittent schedule. Six miles of road that lead to the collecting site are primitive. Inclement weather can cause the road to become impassable. The nature of the road limits access to those who own tough trucks or four-wheel-

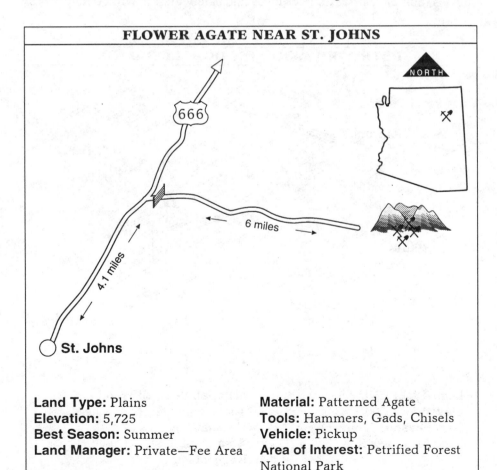

FLOWER AGATE NEAR ST. JOHNS

666

NORTH

6 miles

4.1 miles

St. Johns

Land Type: Plains
Elevation: 5,725
Best Season: Summer
Land Manager: Private—Fee Area

Material: Patterned Agate
Tools: Hammers, Gads, Chisels
Vehicle: Pickup
Area of Interest: Petrified Forest National Park

drive-equipped vehicles.

Richey maintains a supply of the material at his home in St. Johns. Richey blasts the agate loose from its massive seam. Some pieces will show the fracturing that is characteristic of blasted rock. Many of the chunks liberated from the seam will be much too large for lapidary use. Collectors who visit the Richey claims will find that their collecting opportunities are improved if they carry along heavy hammers and gads and chisels. Leather gloves and protective eyewear are advised. The collecting area is located four miles north of St. Johns on U.S. 666 and six miles east on the primitive road.

To obtain permission to collect, contact Reginald Richey, 2nd W. 6th N., St. Johns, AZ 85936, or call (602) 337-4596. The shop he operates from his home is located on the road leading to the St. Johns landfill. Watch for a gray home protected by a gate. A sign on the gate identifies the house as the Richey residence. It is advisable to make collecting or visiting arrangements beforehand.

Lapidaries may encounter problems with some of the agate. The black areas, particularly, tend to undercut. Those who own and use diamond units will minimize the undercutting problem. Those who use silicon carbide units should avoid the coarse wheel and the coarse sander, as these tend to pull the fibers and cause undercutting. Begin the grinding and begin the sanding using a medium grit such as 220. Proceed through the 600 sander and finish with tin or cerium oxide on leather or canvas.

SITE 26: *BANDED ONYX SOUTH OF MAYER*

A substantial deposit of red, white, and tan travertine onyx is located a half-mile southeast of Mayer. The onyx occurs in rupture-size boulders (you rupture if you try to lift one) down to cobbles. Nearly all show a similar pattern, a multicolored brown background interrupted by cream-colored layers and, at times, bright red accent splashes.

The crust of the material is weathered brown and is uninteresting. The diamond saw is needed to expose the interior aspect. The onyx is scattered over a considerable area. Nearly every collector who comes here leaves with all of the material he can handle.

More good news. The deposit is accessible, located a short distance from the paved highway, U.S. 69, that permits travel between Phoenix and Prescott, via Interstate 17. About any kind of vehicle can take you close to the onyx. A short walk will put you in the center of the deposit.

Not all of the Mayer onyx is equally good. Part of the material is vuggy and colorless. The best is solid and banded and contains the attractive browns, yellows, creams, and reds. A close inspection of the material should allow wise selection.

The onyx area is privately owned and is intermittently worked. To

date the owner has not objected to casual collecting by rockhounds. That could change. Keep an eye out for private property signs.

The Mayer onyx, like onyx from other deposits in one aspect, is marginal material for the cabber. A lack of hardness causes the material to accept a poor polish when traditional lapidary technique is used. The finish is matte or satin at best.

The main use for the Mayer material (and for other onyx) is as rough for bookends, and for carvings and spheres. If you are dedicated to cabbing and your professional pride demands perfection of polish, here is a recipe that might work. The main constituent of travertine onyx is calcite. The material is sometimes called calcite onyx. The calcite content can be attacked by any kind of acid. Use that fact to your advantage. Grind and sand using medium fine grits and finish on a used 600 paper worked wet. Dissolve a few grains of oxalic acid (bad stuff, even poisonous) within tin oxide slurry and use this mixture on canvas.

To reach the Mayer deposit, travel south on Arizona 69 one-half mile from the Mayer turnoff. You will see a pullout leading to a locked gate on the east

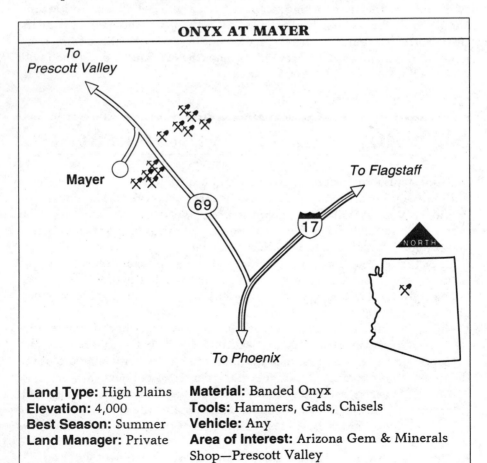

ONYX AT MAYER

To Prescott Valley

Mayer

69

17

To Flagstaff

NORTH

To Phoenix

Land Type: High Plains
Elevation: 4,000
Best Season: Summer
Land Manager: Private

Material: Banded Onyx
Tools: Hammers, Gads, Chisels
Vehicle: Any
Area of Interest: Arizona Gem & Minerals Shop—Prescott Valley

side of the highway. Park here and walk to the east. Even though there is onyx on both sides of the road, the owner does his mining on the west side and you are more apt to encounter owner resistance if you intrude there.

The clay banks that border the south side of Beaver Creek, a mile or so

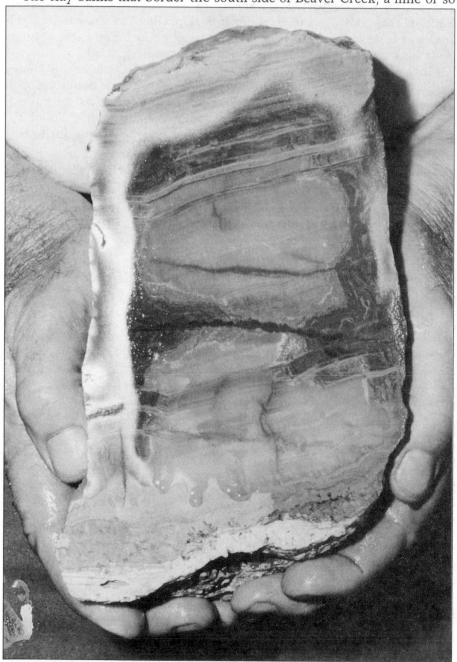

Mayer onyx shows a bold mix of red, yellow, and brown.

SITE 27: AGATE SOUTH OF PERKINSVILLE

A widely distributed field of agate can be found within the Prescott National Forest about six miles south of Perkinsville. The agate is multicolored and is generally free of flaws. The pastel pinks found here, at times containing interesting patterns, are high quality cutting rough.

Much of the public land in the area is leased to the 76 Cattle Ranch. Under the multiple use concept, the area remains open to legitimate public use such as hunting, fishing, and rockhounding. Be a good neighbor as you collect. Leave gates open that you find open and close gates that you find closed. Do not litter and do not attempt to drive on the forest service roads during wet weather. The ruts you leave will be difficult to remove.

The 76 Ranch was founded by prospector James Baker during 1876. The lush graze along the Verde River allowed the herd to prosper—it eventually

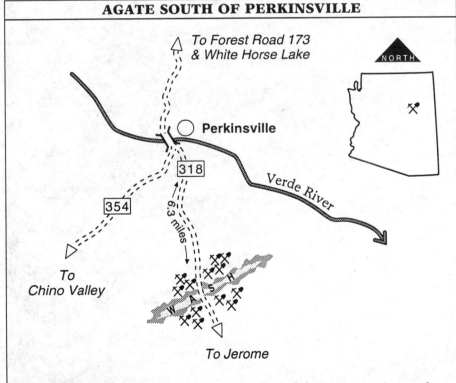

AGATE SOUTH OF PERKINSVILLE

To Forest Road 173 & White Horse Lake

NORTH

Perkinsville

318

354

6.3 miles

Verde River

To Chino Valley

W A S H

To Jerome

Land Type: Pinyon/Juniper Woodlands
Elevation: 3,000
Best Season: Spring, Summer
Land Manager: Prescott National Forest

Material: Agate—various colors
Tools: Rock Pick
Vehicle: Pickup, four-wheelers
Area of Interest: Jerome Mines, White Horse Lake

reached 10,000 head. Baker sold the ranch and the brand to Texas stockman Marion Alexander Perkins in 1900. The ranch has been managed by Perkins descendants since.

At 4,000-feet in elevation, summer and winter temperatures are decent here, with a few exceptions. Those exceptions occur when storm clouds roil from the high country to the north to drop a share of winter rain and snow. If in doubt, check with the Prescott National Forest office at Chino Valley, or the one at Clarkdale, to obtain up-to-date road information. A map of the Prescott National Forest, available at either office, can help you find your way through this immense area of public land.

The collecting area is located about 6.5 miles south of Perkinsville on Forest Road 318. That road, followed to its end, will take you to the carcass of the Jerome area mines. Access to the collecting area can be by Forest Road 318 from the Jerome end or by Forest Road 354 from the Chino Valley end. These roads are narrow dirt that are maintained intermittently, best suited to pickup trucks and other rugged machines.

There is a lot to see within the Prescott National Forest. White Horse Lake, to the north of the collecting area, is a jewel of blue surrounded by grand pine—high country, a summer delight, teeming with elk, mule deer, wild turkey, and nearly every type of critter you can name. Improved campsites are available. Anglers will enjoy the rainbow trout that lurk in the lake.

The Jerome mines are an hour's drive from the agate area. The impressive Sycamore Canyon Wilderness Area is nearby. Rocks, game, and fish—who could ask for more?

SITE 28: *SELENITE NEAR CAMP VERDE*

The clay banks that border the south side of Beaver Creek, a mile or so above its confluence with the Verde River, hold an interesting deposit of fibrous selenite.

The hairlike crystals are snow white and are attached to a gray mudlike material. The hardened mud, with selenite attached, is easily removed using a large mechanics screwdriver as a pry. The fragile nature of the crystals makes them difficult to transport. An empty egg carton does a decent job of housing and protecting the crystals for the trip to the vehicle.

The crystals occur within miniature caves located about two-thirds of the way up the bank. Footing is uncertain; the treacherous nature of the rubble can cause the foot to slip. A nasty fall can be the consequence. Only collectors who are totally fit should collect here.

The Salt Mine near Camp Verde offers a fine opportunity to collect pseudomorphs.

SITE 29: *SALT MINE PSEUDOMORPHS*

The Salt Mine to the south of Camp Verde might be the perfect collecting site. The area is accessible to about any type of vehicle. Summer temperatures are bearable at about one hundred degrees, tops. Winter temperatures often are super. And best of all, the area has been and is a steady supplier of attractive crystal pseudomorphs, in sizes that should interest all collectors.

The most abundant products here are clusters of crystals of gypsum after glauberite. That same glauberite has also been replaced by both calcite and aragonite. Some areas of the mine offer up unaltered glauberite. These crystals are almost always found as singles and are blue-gray. Some are transparent. Do not be alarmed if you notice a gradual transformation as the glauberite is exposed to the air. You are witnessing pseudomorphism in action.

Look for pockets about half-way up the steep banks of the mine to find the glauberite specimens. Although they are singles, as mentioned, many will exhibit a simple twinning.

You will notice a generous assortment of gypsum pseudomorphs after glauberite on the surface. Many of these will be mildly or grossly altered by rain and exposure. Use the rock pick to dig gently into the loose soil to expose sharp specimens. Clean specimens with a dry brush. Use a toothpick to remove clay from hard-to-reach areas. Do not use water.

Some collectors save egg cartons and use these handy containers to hold the somewhat fragile specimens for the trip home. The second best way to transport is to wrap specimens in tissue. When wrapped and carefully packed in a cardboard box, the specimens are likely to survive undamaged.

Summer or winter, the Salt Mine area can be hot. The sun can cause an uncomfortable glare as it reflects from the nearly white soil of the Salt Mine. The use of a good grade of sun screen is recommended.

Summer visitors will be afforded the opportunity to feed a gnat, locally called a "no-see-um." These hungry pests seem most active early and late in the day. An insect repellent containing Deet seems effective in spoiling their appetite.

To reach the Salt Mine area take Interstate 17 to one of the Camp Verde exits. Head south on the Payson Road. At the edge of town, take the Salt Mine

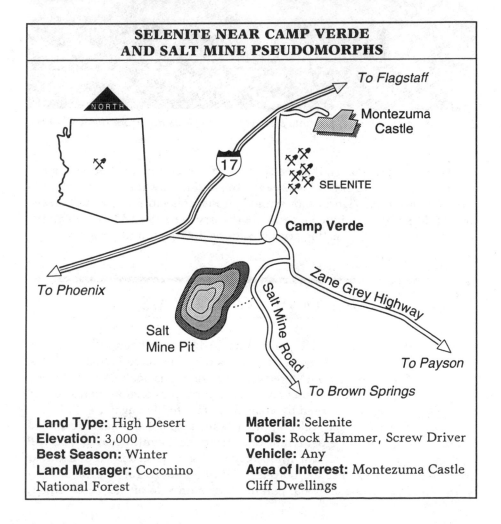

SELENITE NEAR CAMP VERDE AND SALT MINE PSEUDOMORPHS

Land Type: High Desert
Elevation: 3,000
Best Season: Winter
Land Manager: Coconino National Forest

Material: Selenite
Tools: Rock Hammer, Screw Driver
Vehicle: Any
Area of Interest: Montezuma Castle Cliff Dwellings

This sharp pseudomorph (selenite after glauberite) was dug from the wall of the pit.

Road to your right. Follow that road (west and then south) for about two miles and you will see the Salt Mine area to your right. Park there and walk into the collecting area. Vigorous (or semi-vigorous) collectors will want to leave the Salt Mine itself to hike and explore the dry washes and low hills to the west of the mine. Interesting crystallizations may be found here also.

SITE 30: *JASPER AT RODEO FLATS*

Some of the most colorful jasper found in Arizona has been collected from the area of Rodeo Flats. A specimen collected by the noted lapidary Martin Koning of Morristown (and featured on the cover of his book, *Prospecting For Gem Stones In Arizona and the Southwest* is a handsome conglomeration of red and yellow jasper interrupted by areas of a clear to blue agate.

To reach the Rodeo Flat collecting area, take Prescott National Forest Road 574 south from Camp Verde. A mile or so from the downtown area, you will notice the dumps of the Salt Mine to your right. (See description under Collecting Salt Mine Pseudomorphs.) Continue south for fifteen or fifty miles. The road will somewhat parallel the south side of the Verde River.

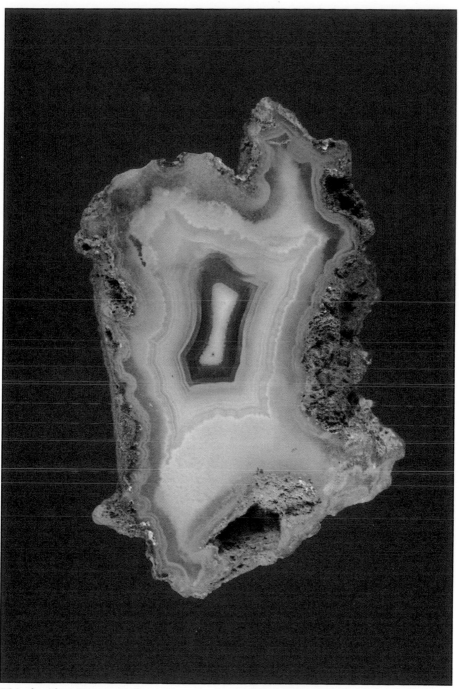

This fortification agate from Fourth of July Butte shows an attractive red center.

Above: *Pedestal logs within a part of the Petrified Forest National Park are revealed as wind and rain erode the soft soil.*
Left: *When cut and polished, petrified wood shows a rainbow of colors.*

This pioneer cabin near the Blue Wilderness Area decays with dignity.

Arizona turquoise comes in a broad range of color and with varying inclusions.

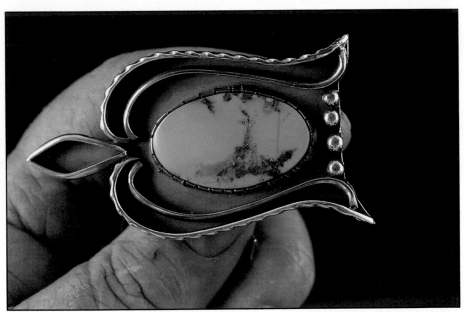

This handsome piece of Bisbee blue turquoise is surrounded by a stylized peyote bird, a figure of religious significance to the Navajo people.

Above: *Rain runoff seeping through the dump at the old United Verde Mine in Jerome takes on the green color of copper ores.*

Left: *Many Arizona copper mines produce the copper carbonate azurite, shown here in roseate form.*

Newspaper Rock within Petrified Forest National Park is covered with petroglyphs like these.

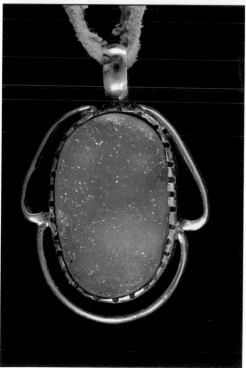

Above: This stunning quartz and copper cooperation came from a massive pocket within the Live Oak Shaft of the Miami-Inspiration property near Globe. *Left:* A druse quartz coat over the copper mineral chrysocolla can be eye catching. This specimen is from the Miami-Inspiration property.

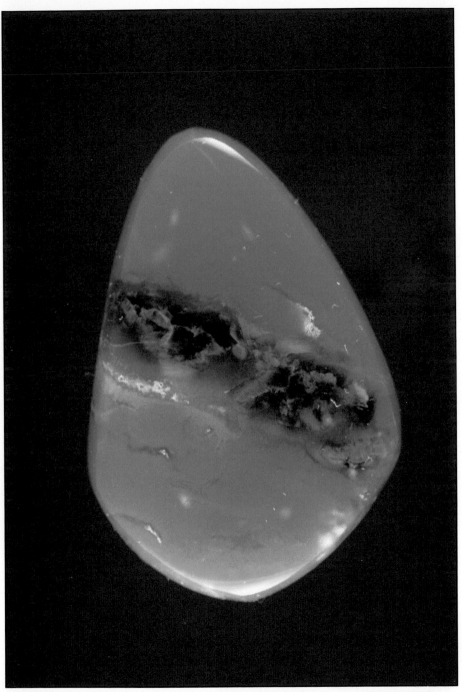

Chalcedony colored by the complex copper chrysocolla can be a dandy find. The green band is enclosed malachite. This specimen is from the Miami-Inspiration property.

Rodeo Flats will be seen to the east of the road. The jasper can be found by searching to the right (west) of this primitive road. Walk downhill, watching as you walk. Some of the jasper will be found as float on the side hill and at the bottom of the hill.

Hunt the east side of the road (Rodeo Flats) to the Verde River to find chalcedony after aragonite pseudomorphs.

A mile or two farther east you will find a locked gate that leads to the cattle ranch buildings at Brown Springs. Park here (off the road) and walk to hunt

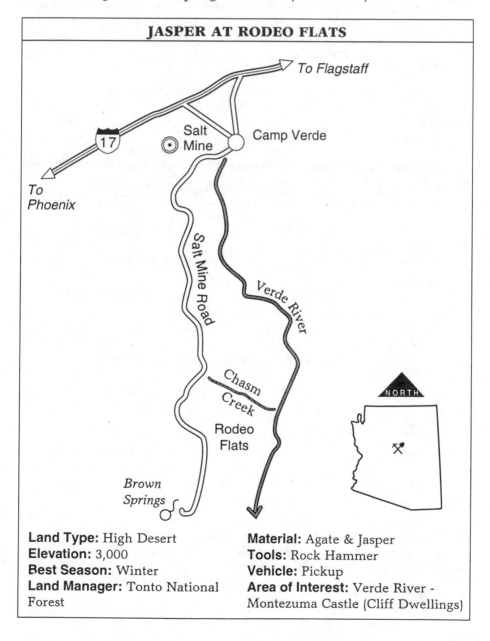

JASPER AT RODEO FLATS

Land Type: High Desert
Elevation: 3,000
Best Season: Winter
Land Manager: Tonto National Forest

Material: Agate & Jasper
Tools: Rock Hammer
Vehicle: Pickup
Area of Interest: Verde River - Montezuma Castle (Cliff Dwellings)

the low hills that surround the area. Interesting agate in the form of float can be found.

The area between Brown Springs and the power plant at Childs, a distance of about ten rugged miles (nearly all of it roadless), is an area that should produce a variety of agate and jasper, according to Koning. Both sides of the river should be equally productive.

The last few miles to road's end at Brown Springs can be hard on a passenger car. Tough trucks, or some other kind of beefed up vehicle, are advised. Those who have a hankering to hike downriver to explore should know that the country is rugged. Summertime temperatures exceed the 100-degree mark nearly every day. The big and bad kind of rattlesnake called the western diamondback hangs out here, mostly undisturbed. It is not the kind of country one would pick for a casual stroll.

The jasper and agate from this area present no exceptional cutting problems. Grind and sand through 600 grit and polish on leather or canvas using tin or cerium oxide.

SITE 31: *CONCRETIONS NEAR PAYSON*

An easily accessible site split by Forest Road 64, locally called The Control Road, offers an interesting kind of rock, balls of a coarsely crystalline material locally called "Brainstone" or "Septarian Nodules." Some collectors have reported finding hollow nodules (geodes) containing crystal centers. Such finds are rare with this material. The main worth of the nodules is as specimens. The interior is dull and uninteresting.

Nodule size will range from marble size up to softball size. A few are larger. All exhibit the typical boytroidal crust. Color will range from dirty white to dark brown. A similar material can be found about a mile south and a mile west of the Payson Country Club. Both areas offer an opportunity to collect agate of varying color. The purchase of a Tonto National Forest map from the Forest Service office at Payson will make it easy to navigate.

SITE 32: *QUARTZ CRYSTALS AT DIAMOND POINT*

The area southwest of the Diamond Point Lookout has been a stingy but steady producer of clear quartz terminations. Even though countless collectors have peered at the ground until their eyeballs ached, and even though those countless collectors have stooped to retrieve every scrap of clear quartz, heavy summer rains (locally called the monsoons) continue to expose a fresh crop of faceting grade quartz.

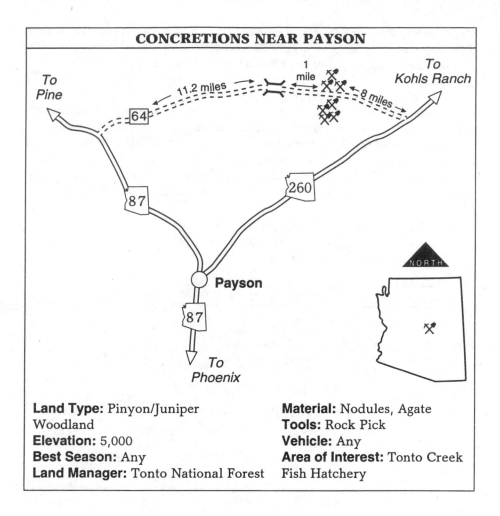

CONCRETIONS NEAR PAYSON

Land Type: Pinyon/Juniper Woodland
Elevation: 5,000
Best Season: Any
Land Manager: Tonto National Forest

Material: Nodules, Agate
Tools: Rock Pick
Vehicle: Any
Area of Interest: Tonto Creek Fish Hatchery

The crystals have formed as a guest within limestone pockets. Nearly all are terminations with no prism. Some show the doubly terminated form of the fine quartz crystal terminations from Herkimer County, New York.

Collectors who put a low sun to their back will find it less difficult to spot the sometimes inconspicuous crystals. Early morning and late evening are the prime collecting times. Walk slowly and scan the area for a few feet out front. An examination of digging dumps left by previous collectors sometimes produces a prize. If you are into digging, you will need gads, chisels, and heavy hammers, because the host rock is tough. Heavy gloves and eye protectors are recommended.

Quartz crystal terminations can be found at other locations within the area. The author has collected crystals from many of the low hills that border the south side of Tonto National Forest Road between the Diamond Point Lookout to the east and the Little Diamond Rim to the west. A number of primitive forest service roads and trails leave Forest Road 64, locally called

The Control Road, to lead to interesting areas. On one visit, the author discovered a termination as large as Rambo's fist. The base of the termination was feathery grading to a glassy tip. The point of the termination was tinted a delicate amethyst.

This entire area offers pleasant summer collecting. The mile-high elevation provides comfortable daytime temperatures. Many Forest Service campgrounds provide camping space. Nearby streams, such as Tonto, Christopher, and the East Verde River are stocked with rainbow trout from the fish hatchery upstream from Kohls Ranch. Midway between Kohls Ranch and the hatchery is the reconstructed cabin of the author Zane Grey. Grey stayed there when he came to the area to hunt lion and bear. The cabin was his domicile when he wrote "Under the Tonto Rim." In actuality he was under the Mogollon Rim, but he used artistic license.

A detailed map of the Tonto National Forest (available at ranger headquarters in Payson) can greatly assist navigation.

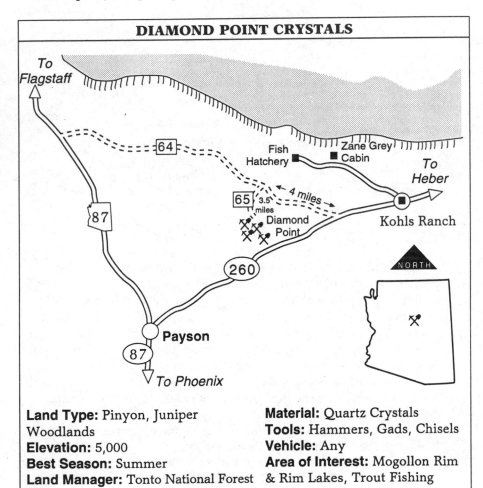

DIAMOND POINT CRYSTALS

Land Type: Pinyon, Juniper Woodlands
Elevation: 5,000
Best Season: Summer
Land Manager: Tonto National Forest

Material: Quartz Crystals
Tools: Hammers, Gads, Chisels
Vehicle: Any
Area of Interest: Mogollon Rim & Rim Lakes, Trout Fishing

SITE 33: *AGATES & FOSSILS NEAR KOHLS RANCH*

The fine-grained jasper found here consists of alternating bands of white and gray, which locals call "Zebra Agate." The jasper occurs as float over a wide area that seems centered near the community of Christopher Creek.

This is Arizona high country. Ponderosa pine at the higher elevations degrades to string bark juniper and Gambel's oak lower down. A pair of pristine streams attracts trout fishermen to the area. There are numerous national forest campgrounds, above and below the 2,000-foot-high Mogollon Rim. Rim country lakes, such as Woods Canyon and Blue Ridge, provide fishing and camping through the summer months.

The same area that delivers the striped jasper also offers a number of interesting fossils. Brachiopod fossils can be found exposed by highway cuts near the junction of Arizona 260 and Forest Road 64 (The Control Road), a few miles to the southwest of Kohls Ranch.

A smaller brach, sometimes partially replaced by a red chalcedony, can be found near the R-C (that's the R Bar C) Boy Scout ranch. A fossil of a different type can be found atop the rim. Fine brachiopod casts, preserved in limestone, can be found on the rocky points that overlook the rim escarpment.

The most attractive fossil in the area is a finely detailed ossification of a somewhat large (several inches across) coral. A profusion of small crinoid stems is scattered over the low hills north and east of the East Verde Bridge on Arizona 87. Travel north of the bridge until you see a pullout to the left. You will see a small fenced plot containing a pair of graves (locally called Holder's Grave). Park here and hunt the low hills to the opposite side of the road. You will need to look closely. The fossils are small, the largest having about the diameter of a soda straw. Some are as much as one inch long. The

Above left: *Zebra agate, actually a jasper, is scattered over a wide area bisected by Christopher Creek.* **Above right:** *Fossil coral is plentiful along the low hills beneath the Mogollon Rim.*

color of the fossil closely matches the ground color. Thus camouflaged, they can be difficult to sight.

The entire area that extends from Payson north to Holbrook and from Holbrook west to the Hualapai Indian Reservation is a part of the Mississippian Redwall Limestone. The ridges of this Paleozoic formation are fossil-rich. Many of the fossils were laid down when shallow seas inundated the area. Unfortunately, the fossils often remain encased in a tenacious limestone. Even so, the patient collector willing to spend time and effort will be rewarded with many interesting finds.

Much of the area is located within the Tonto, Coconino, and Kaibab national forests. Detailed maps, available at moderate cost, show Forest Service roads and prominent geologic features. Nearly any Forest Service office within the area will stock the maps.

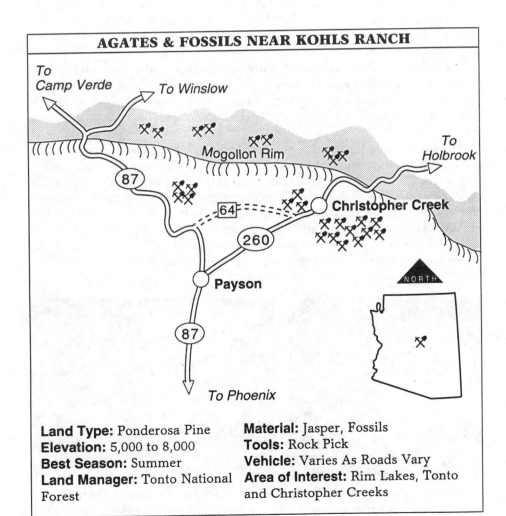

AGATES & FOSSILS NEAR KOHLS RANCH

Land Type: Ponderosa Pine
Elevation: 5,000 to 8,000
Best Season: Summer
Land Manager: Tonto National Forest

Material: Jasper, Fossils
Tools: Rock Pick
Vehicle: Varies As Roads Vary
Area of Interest: Rim Lakes, Tonto and Christopher Creeks

SITE 34: *PERIDOT AT SAN CARLOS*

Peridot of excellent quality can be found within the cavities of the basaltic rock that forms Peridot Mesa. The mesa is a part of the San Carlos Apache Indian Reservation, and the beautiful green stone is mined as a tribal enterprise. **Collecting by non-reservation residents is prohibited.** Rough and faceted peridot is available for purchase at stores located within the town of San Carlos, the tribal headquarters. In some instances, tumbled stones have been drilled and strung as necklaces.

The ban on non-Indian collecting is relatively recent. As recently as about twenty years ago, non-Indians were allowed to collect after paying a modest fee. At one point during the 1970s, the tribe contracted with a non-Indian firm so that the peridot could be mined and marketed.

As of this writing, individual Apaches work the basalt to discover the pods and masses of peridot within the basalt cavities. Much of the material

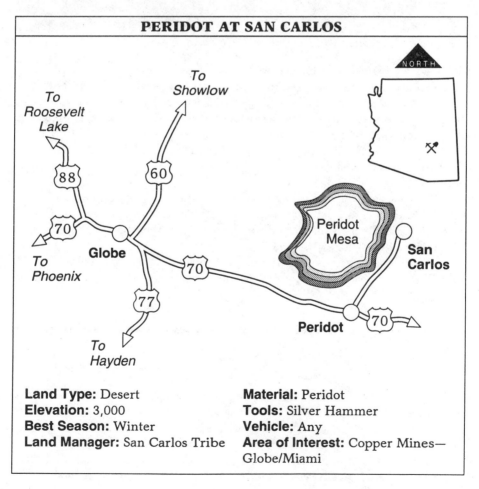

PERIDOT AT SAN CARLOS

Land Type: Desert
Elevation: 3,000
Best Season: Winter
Land Manager: San Carlos Tribe

Material: Peridot
Tools: Silver Hammer
Vehicle: Any
Area of Interest: Copper Mines—Globe/Miami

When cut, this peridot will yield several five-carat stones.

recovered is coarsely crystalline. Some contains clear peridot, but of pinhead size. Occasionally peridot is found that weighs several dozen carats in the rough. A faceted stone of five carats is considered extraordinary. Stones weighing up to ten carats have been faceted from the San Carlos material. Such stones are rare and exceedingly valuable. Flagg, in his *Minerals of Arizona*, (University of Arizona Press 1959) mentions that a cut stone from the San Carlos deposit weighed 25.75 carats, but gives no further information.

Collectors wanting up-to-date information on collecting opportunities on the San Carlos Apache Indian Reservation should contact the San Carlos Apache Tribe, Recreation & Wildlife Department, P.O. Box 97, San Carlos, AZ 85550; phone (602) 475-2653.

As previously noted, policies governing non-Indian use of tribal land is set by tribal councils. As the council members change, so might the policy change.

SITE 35: *GARNETS AT STANLEY BUTTE*

The andradite garnets found at Stanley Butte are almost surely the best specimen garnets found in the state. The splendent crystal groups are often a green-tinted brown. Crystals to two inches have been found. The host rock, much of the time, is a tenacious, massive garnet.

The deposit is on land owned by the San Carlos Apache Tribe. **At this writing, the Apaches have closed the entire area to entry.** As was noted in the chapter about peridot, collecting regulations can change within any purview. A letter or a telephone call to the tribal recreation division should reveal current policy.

Collecting garnet specimens at Stanley Butte is hard work. The garnets crowd small cavities that interrupt the garnet-influenced country rock. A cracking hammer and a gad or heavy-duty chisel are the minimum tools needed. Sledge hammers and picks are even better, in many cases.

The reward can be worth the effort. Many of the crystal clusters are classic. Many show an uncommon interior sheen, perhaps because of an iron oxide inclusion. Specimens from some pockets share space with fine doubly terminated quartz crystals (up to one-half foot long). Some single crystals of garnet are nearly transparent, although no faceting grade crystals have been reported, and may be green or gold.

Stanley Butte is located about twenty-five miles south-southeast of the town of San Carlos and about fifteen miles south-southwest of the town of Bylas. To the east sits 8,000-foot Mount Turnbull. A primitive reservation road leads to the site.

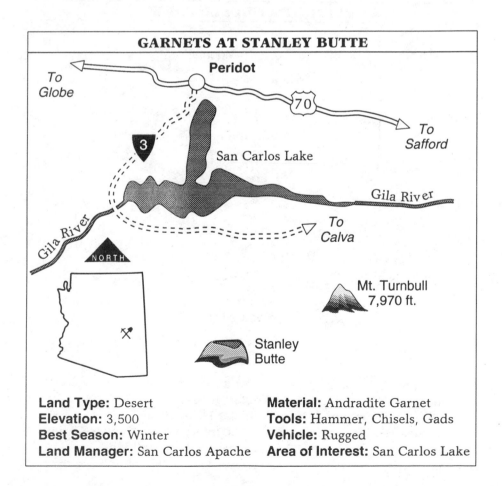

GARNETS AT STANLEY BUTTE

To Globe

Peridot

70

To Safford

3

San Carlos Lake

Gila River

To Calva

Gila River

NORTH

Mt. Turnbull
7,970 ft.

Stanley Butte

Land Type: Desert
Elevation: 3,500
Best Season: Winter
Land Manager: San Carlos Apache

Material: Andradite Garnet
Tools: Hammer, Chisels, Gads
Vehicle: Rugged
Area of Interest: San Carlos Lake

SITE 36: *PERIDOT AT BUELL PARK*

The peridot found near Buell Park differs radically from the peridot found near the San Carlos Apache town of the same name. The Apache material, as noted in "Peridot at San Carlos," is recovered as the content of "volcanic bombs." Much of the San Carlos material is fractured and has feathery flaws. The Buell Park peridot is found as weathered float. The interior is often clean and brilliant, with few internal flaws.

A yellow kind of the chrysolite (forsterite) has been found within the Buell Park deposit. The absence of iron apparently causes the yellow aspect. Sometimes this gem shows a pale green flash.

A brown variety of the chrysolite (fayalite) also has been found. Even though brown is seldom a coveted color for facetors, fayalite can be turned to a gorgeous gem when properly faceted.

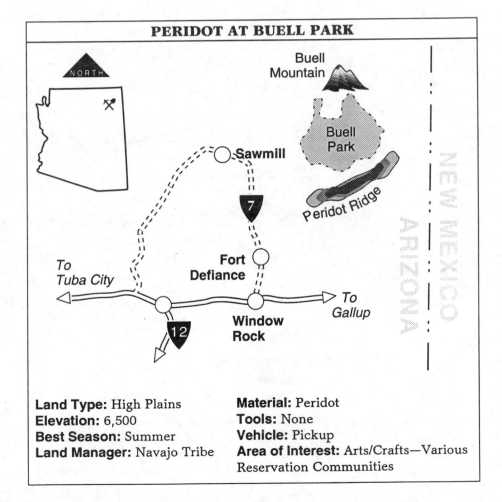

PERIDOT AT BUELL PARK

Land Type: High Plains
Elevation: 6,500
Best Season: Summer
Land Manager: Navajo Tribe

Material: Peridot
Tools: None
Vehicle: Pickup
Area of Interest: Arts/Crafts—Various Reservation Communities

The Buell Park peridot occurs within an ancient volcanic caldera, now badly eroded. One geologist who has viewed the area has called the caldera the largest deposit of kimberlite (yep, that's the stuff that carries the diamond) in the world.

Buell Park is located on the Navajo Indian Reservation, about sixteen miles north of the tribal headquarters at Window Rock and about five miles east of the town of Sawmill. The park (in the West nearly any meadow area can be called a park) is bordered by Buell Mountain, elevation 8,171 feet, to the north and by Peridot Ridge to the south. Take Reservation Road 7 through Fort Defiance and toward Sawmill. A series of primitive roads (bad in wet weather) leaves Navajo 7 about a mile south of Sawmill and leads northeast to the park. Peridots can be found on the flats slightly beyond the powerline that crosses the park.

Current collecting status is fuzzy. The peridot deposit is a long way from nowhere. Rather than risk a long trip and be turned away, **collectors are advised to contact the office of the Navajo Tribal Rangers to ascertain current regulations.**

SITE 37: *PYROPE GARNETS ON THE NAVAJO RESERVATION*

Brilliant red pyrope garnets can be found on Garnet Ridge and on Comb Ridge within the immensity of the Navajo Indian Reservation. Each of the areas is nearly contiguous and each is likely a separate instance of the same outcrop.

Because small garnets are sometimes found as a component of ant hills, some locals insist that the garnets are "mined" from deep underground and brought to the surface by the industrious ants. Logic suggests otherwise. Only smallish garnets are found around the ant hills. Larger garnets, up to the size of a large green pea, often are found.

Peridots occasionally are found associated with the garnets, just as garnets are sometimes found among the peridots at Buell Park. No garnets examined by the author showed a crystal face. None exceeded one-quarter inch in diameter. Even so, the color and clarity of these blood-red bits of glassy garnet have caused some to call them "the best doggone pyropes in the world."

In a time long past, red garnet was a coveted gem rough. Local Navajos spent a good deal of their free time scouring the ridges. A good garnet might bring a reward of several dollars. The garnet jewelry fad, sad to say, ran its course, and the price dropped drastically.

Many Navajo garnets are about BB size. A few approach one-quarter inch in diameter. A monster that was more than an inch across once was found.

Comb Ridge is an east-west ridge that roughly parallels Navajo Highway 64 between Kayenta and Mexican Water, a distance of about fifty desolate miles. To the north are El Capitan, Agathla, The Mittens, and the other stark red spires that cooperate to form the picturesque Monument Valley.

Even though Garnet Ridge does not appear on current maps, the ridge is centered about five miles due west of the Mexican Water Trading Post, according to sources. If that is so, Garnet Ridge is a north-reaching ridge that connects to the east end of Comb Ridge.

Although garnets can be found in several places on Comb Ridge, they reportedly are particularly plentiful about ten miles north of Mexican Water near Moses Rock and Mule Ears. Current collecting status is hazy. Some collectors report having been allowed to collect garnets on a casual or hobby basis. Others have said they were asked to leave the area by Navajo Tribal Rangers. **Hounds who hope to collect in the area are advised to contact the office of The Navajo Tribal Rangers at Window Rock for up-to-date policy.**

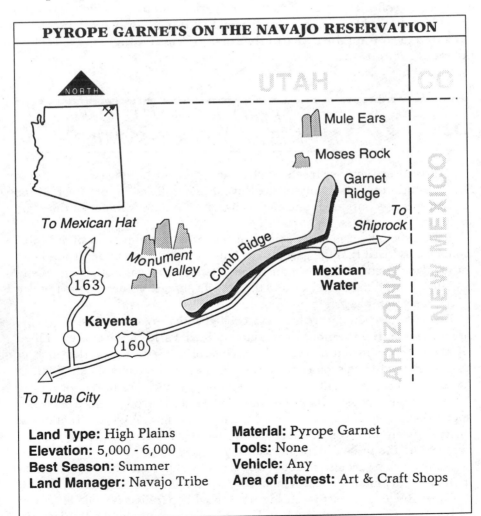

PYROPE GARNETS ON THE NAVAJO RESERVATION

Land Type: High Plains
Elevation: 5,000 - 6,000
Best Season: Summer
Land Manager: Navajo Tribe

Material: Pyrope Garnet
Tools: None
Vehicle: Any
Area of Interest: Art & Craft Shops

SITE 38: *AGATE AT LIMESTONE GULCH*

The agates of Limestone Gulch are among the best in Arizona, perhaps the world. The best material here is a fortification agate that shows snowy white centers surrounded by royal purple. Other nodules will have the purple replaced by a delicate lavender. Many of the "potatoes" contain alternating bands of white and gray.

The nodule exterior is a dirty white and is often rough, effectively disguising the beauty that may be within. The agate "makes" in a tough rhyolite. Collectors who have the proper tools-gads, chisels, heavy hammers, and picks—and the will can sometimes recover nodules up to fist size.

The float material has been hard hit. Many out-of-state collectors visit regularly in an effort to add a quality specimen or two to the collection. Clifton-area rockhounds—and there are a good many of them—head for Mulligan Peak after each hard rain, hoping to have first chance at the nodules that may have been exposed. Agate nodules can be found on the northeast

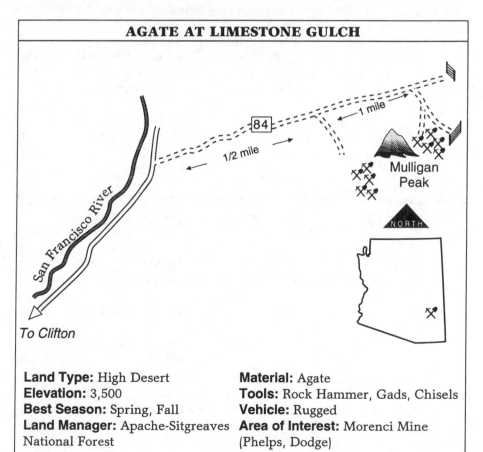

AGATE AT LIMESTONE GULCH

San Francisco River

84

1/2 mile

1 mile

Mulligan Peak

NORTH

To Clifton

Land Type: High Desert
Elevation: 3,500
Best Season: Spring, Fall
Land Manager: Apache-Sitgreaves National Forest

Material: Agate
Tools: Rock Hammer, Gads, Chisels
Vehicle: Rugged
Area of Interest: Morenci Mine (Phelps, Dodge)

and southwest slopes of Mulligan Peak. Collectors who walk away from the road—those who work hardest—will have the best luck.

Even though the mean elevation within the collecting area is about a mile high, mid-summer temperatures can be uncomfortably hot. Mid-winter temperatures can be uncomfortably cold. Spring and fall are about right.

Limestone Gulch and Mulligan Peak are located on land administered by the Apache-Sitgreaves National Forest. An inexpensive forest map, available at the Forest Service office in Clifton, can be helpful.

The Forest Service road that leads to the deposit follows Limestone Gulch and is often rough. Up-to-date information on road condition can be obtained from Forest Service folks. They will tell you, often, that the primitive nature of the road limits access to four-wheel-drive vehicles. The road will take you to within walking distance of the agate deposit.

These tips might make your experience with the Limestone Gulch agate trouble free: Walk and watch carefully, keeping an eye peeled for a small piece of agate crust peeking through the soil. Often the largest and most brilliantly colored nodules are found this way. Resist the temptation to use the rock pick to chip a window so that you may have a quick look at the hidden interior. Such chipping almost always causes cutting problems in the form of internal fracturing. Do not disdain chips and naturally fractured bits of quality material. Cut free-form, these partial nodules can turn into handsome cabochons. To obtain a truly striking cabochon from a small nodule, use the grinder to abrade away the crust, following the contour of the nodule. When the purple band has been exposed, grind through at the top to expose the white interior.

The Limestone Gulch material is agate and should be worked just as you would any other agate; that is, grind and sand through 600 grit and polish on leather or canvas with tin or cerium oxide.

SITE 39: *APACHE TEARS NEAR SUPERIOR*

The perlite mine that produces the obsidian nodules known as "Apache Tears" sits near the flank of Picket Post Mountain. A band of Apache Indians, legend has it, were chased to the sheer cliffs by the cavalry. Rather than surrender or risk capture, the warriors rode their horses over the cliff and dropped several hundred feet to a certain death. The widows and girlfriends eventually came to the cliff edge to wail and cry, as was the custom. A compassionate god saw their misery and turned their tears to stone so that the bravery of the warriors and the love of the women would be forever remembered.

Apache Tear Caves, a commercial operation, allows fee collecting. The charge is modest and the tears are plentiful. Bulldozers blade off the perlite to expose fresh tears so there is always a plentiful supply. The obsidian

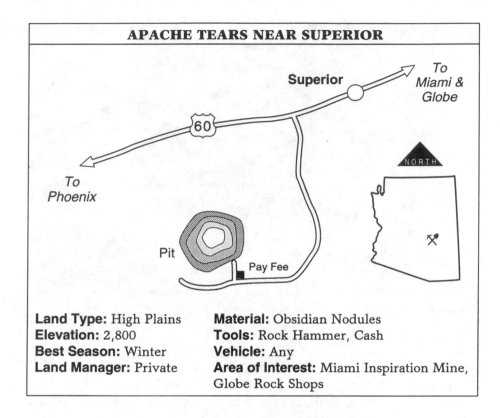

APACHE TEARS NEAR SUPERIOR

Superior

To Miami & Globe

60

To Phoenix

NORTH

Pit

Pay Fee

Land Type: High Plains
Elevation: 2,800
Best Season: Winter
Land Manager: Private

Material: Obsidian Nodules
Tools: Rock Hammer, Cash
Vehicle: Any
Area of Interest: Miami Inspiration Mine, Globe Rock Shops

nodules are glassy and have a smoke tint. Size will range from pea size to about the size of an extra large egg. Many collectors make it a point to collect specimens of obsidian that are connected to the perlite matrix to use as display pieces.

The obsidian here is particularly attractive. The perlite matrix has protected the semi-soft obsidian from weathering. The somewhat rough rind is pocked and is pleasingly splendent.

Do not attempt to grind or slab these tears. They contain internal stresses that may cause them to fracture or shatter. It is best to tumble the tears first to remove the stress and then proceed with the modifications.

Lapidaries who attempt to cut cabochons from the Apache Tears will almost certainly be disappointed. The interior is mostly smokey glass, sometimes containing a bit of darker banding. Other obsidians look much better in the cab case.

Tumbling can turn the tears into attractive baroques. The right recipe can turn the tears into a multitude of black marbles. Obtaining that perfect polish can be tricky. The somewhat soft nature of the tears can make the process frustrating. Here is a recipe that will work. Tumble rough tears in a slurry of 80 grit and baking soda for about one week. Rinse tears and tumbler and tumble in a slurry of 220 grit for six or seven days. Clean and tumble in #4F grit for about five days. Clean up and tumble, using mud and filler. Apply

Proper tumbling can turn the Superior "tears" into attractive baroques.

initial polish using sugar, rice hulls, filler, and titanium, tumbling for a couple of days. Use rice hulls, sugar, filler, and detergent to put on the final polish. This final step will take about forty-eight hours.

The Apache Tear Caves are easy to find. Travel about a mile southwest of Superior on U.S. 60 until you see the Apache Tear Caves sign. Turn left and drive the mile-and-a-half to the area.

SITE 40: MARBLE IN THE SUPERSTITION MOUNTAINS

Rockers who like to mess around with marble will find this rough country deposit interesting. The marble here is fine-grained and polishes about as well as most marble. The color is mostly mixtures of reds and greens.

Only collectors who ride about in a four-wheel-drive vehicle should visit here. Forest Service Road 172 leading to the deposit is only occasionally maintained. That, and the fact that the road follows the course of a canyon for much of the way, causes rough going.

The Superstition Mountains, the legendary location of The Lost Dutchman Mine, can be seen to the northwest. A place or two will provide a peek at Weaver's Needle, an important landmark to those who chase the legend. Do not succumb to gold fever and head for the gold at a dead run. The Superstitions are dangerous during the best season, winter, and can be deadly during the worst season, summer. A good many folks have lost their lives while hunting a treasure that quite likely does not exist. The red and green marble is about all of the treasure the Superstitions hold.

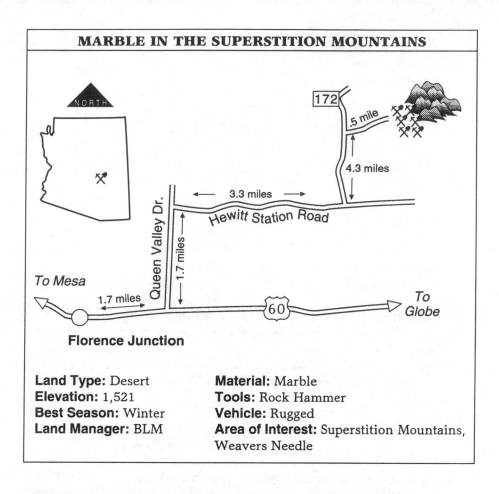

MARBLE IN THE SUPERSTITION MOUNTAINS

NORTH

172

.5 mile

4.3 miles

3.3 miles

Queen Valley Dr.

Hewitt Station Road

1.7 miles

To Mesa

1.7 miles

60

To Globe

Florence Junction

Land Type: Desert
Elevation: 1,521
Best Season: Winter
Land Manager: BLM

Material: Marble
Tools: Rock Hammer
Vehicle: Rugged
Area of Interest: Superstition Mountains, Weavers Needle

SITE 41: *THE ARIZONA AGATE MINE*

The Arizona Agate Mine is located near the west part of a rough piece of real estate called Bloody Basin. The basin was so named, according to some accounts, because a marauding band of Apaches ambushed a mine supply wagon down on the Hassayampa, killing men and livestock and stealing some supplies. The tracks led northeast. A grumpy posse gave chase to get even. A band of about 100 Apaches was discovered within the area now called Bloody Basin. Even though no good evidence existed to show that these were the unfriendlies, the posse figured they would do. The band was annihilated in a bloody encounter.

Bloody Basin is one of the more remote areas in Arizona. A few ranchers run semi-wild cattle here. The area occasionally is visited by hunters, after the wild deer, javelina, mountain lion, bobcat, and coyote, and by hounds who hunt the wild jasper and the wild agate. Otherwise, the area is pristine

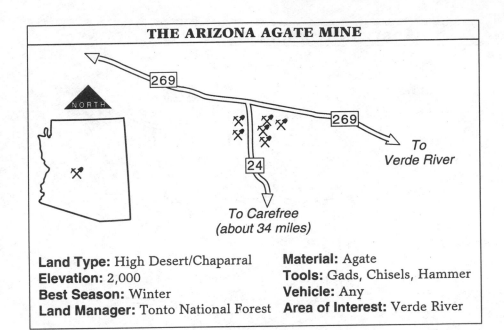

THE ARIZONA AGATE MINE

Land Type: High Desert/Chaparral
Elevation: 2,000
Best Season: Winter
Land Manager: Tonto National Forest

Material: Agate
Tools: Gads, Chisels, Hammer
Vehicle: Any
Area of Interest: Verde River

and lonely. As recently as 1949, a family became lost within the area and nearly froze before they became unlost. (It can get cold in the wintertime but usually does not.)

The Arizona Agate Mine is located near the junction of Tonto National Forest Road 24, leading south to Cave Creek, and Forest Road 269, leading west to Interstate 17 and east to the Verde River at Sheeps Bridge.

The agate mined here was some of the best in Arizona. The material was of two general types. A red and yellow plume surrounded by clear agate and a yellow or red moss (sometimes combined) in the clear agate. Do not expect to find this type of material as float. Although there is some agate float available, its quality is inferior. The best material is buried. The seam worked by the Arizona Agate Mine pretty much pinched out.

Other agate seams are available to collectors willing to trade sweat for it. Bring along heavy tools, picks, shovels, bars, gads, and hammers. You will work hard for every quality piece of rough. Often the effort is well rewarded.

SITE 42: *PURPLE AGATE NEAR SHEEPS BRIDGE*

The person who wrote the song "Forty Miles of Bad Road" must have recently traveled the road leading from Interstate 17 to the Verde River. It is almost exactly forty miles and much of the road is bad; typical backcountry dirt, wide enough for one-way traffic through much of its course. A number of interesting rock-collecting sites are located close to this primitive road.

Collectors who travel to road's end hoping to view Sheep's Bridge are doomed to disappointment. The bridge, built for sheepmen to herd the flock across the river during the annual march to the high country, was dynamited at the request of officials of the Tonto National Forest because the bridge was in disrepair and there was no money available to reconstruct. The sheep will not be inconvenienced; they now ride within huge stock trucks. The journey that once took weeks now is accomplished within hours.

A deposit of purple agate, sometimes containing sagenite, is located west of the former site of Sheep's Bridge. The site is atop the mesa, before the road starts the final descent to the river. Watch for a low hill to the left (north) of the road. An old ruin will be on the hill crest. The agate seams, and some float, will be along the base of that hill.

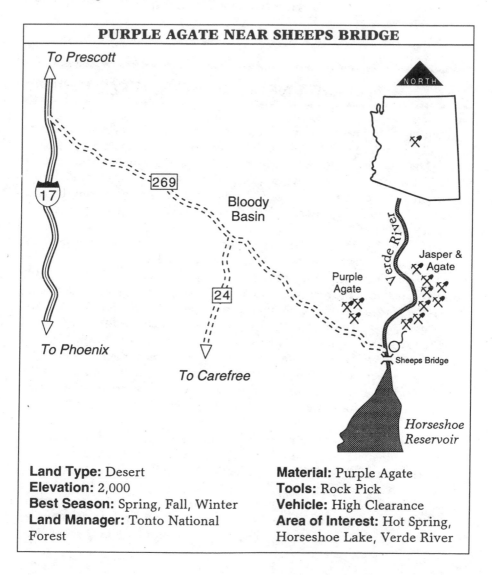

PURPLE AGATE NEAR SHEEPS BRIDGE

Land Type: Desert
Elevation: 2,000
Best Season: Spring, Fall, Winter
Land Manager: Tonto National Forest

Material: Purple Agate
Tools: Rock Pick
Vehicle: High Clearance
Area of Interest: Hot Spring, Horseshoe Lake, Verde River

Other agate and jasper deposits are located on the east side of the Verde (Spanish for green) River. With the bridge gone, you will find it necessary to get your feet wet to reach the east side. The low hills that border the upstream often carry interesting examples of both agate and jasper.

As a further inducement (as if one were needed), a genuine hot spring sits on the west side of the Verde River a bit upstream from where the bridge used to be. The author and a companion once camped close to the river while enjoying an extended rock hunt. A passing cowboy shared the campfire and told of the hot spring. Old time cowboys, he said, had hauled a washtub to the spring and placed it so that the hot (actually, comfortably warm) water would flow through. The spring was found, with bath tub in place, and the two hot hounds enjoyed many a bath, granted privacy by the tall reeds that grew around the spring. A Tonto National Forest map will facilitate travel within this area.

SITE 43: *AGATE NEAR HORSESHOE RESERVOIR*

A variety of interesting agate and jasper can be found scattered among a group of pale hills near Horseshoe Dam. The best of the material has black and red cooperating to form a flashy chunk of rough. Much of the material here is snow white. Some shows the gray color some folks call blue. The agate appears to occur over a large area. Collectors who walk away from the road are most likely to find the best and the most material. Jasper of varying color also can be found.

Humboldt Mountain can be seen about five miles to the west of this part of Horseshoe Reservoir. And although the author has not made personal investigation, he suspects that interesting gem rough can be found within the entire area between the reservoir and the mountain. A well-maintained road, Forest Road 562, leads to the mountain from the east. Take Forest Road 205 east from Cave Creek (also called Horseshoe Dam Road) for about seven miles. The road will split. Forest Road 19 goes east to Bartlett Dam. Stay on Forest Road 205 for about another nine miles until you come to the home of the Salt River Project employee who tends the dam (sometimes called the dam guy). A flat area a bit south of the dam guy's house has given up good agate in the past. More agate can be found by hiking to the pale hills to the west.

Both Horseshoe Reservoir and Bartlett Lake offer the opportunity to fish for largemouth bass, crappie, channel and flathead catfish, and bluegill perch. The Verde River offers excellent opportunities for both kinds of catfish.

As previously noted, the map prepared by the folks from Tonto National Forest can be a navigational help. Rockers who hound Arizona, as a matter of fact, will want to own at least one each of the national forest maps.

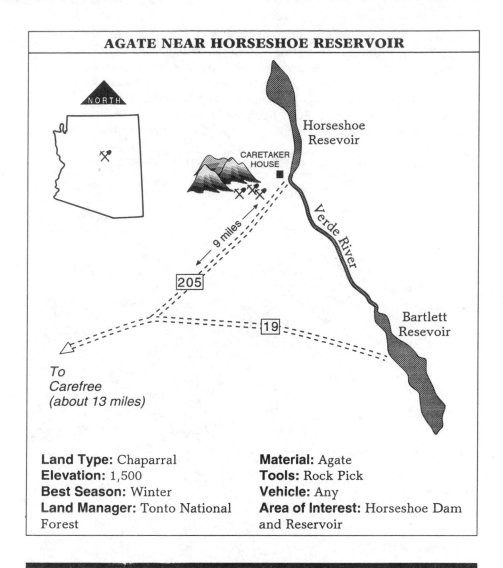

AGATE NEAR HORSESHOE RESERVOIR

NORTH

Horseshoe
Resevoir

CARETAKER
HOUSE

Verde River

9 miles

205

19

Bartlett
Resevoir

To
Carefree
(about 13 miles)

Land Type: Chaparral
Elevation: 1,500
Best Season: Winter
Land Manager: Tonto National
Forest

Material: Agate
Tools: Rock Pick
Vehicle: Any
Area of Interest: Horseshoe Dam
and Reservoir

SITE 44: *JASPER & ONYX NORTH OF CAREFREE*

At one time, a beautifully mottled red jasper locally called "Poppy Jasper" littered the ground west of Cave Creek. Collectors from all parts of the country came to get their share. Some took more than their share. But no one was concerned. The tons of material scattered over a wide area convinced everyone that the collecting bonanza would last forever. It did not. All, or nearly all, of that handsome material has disappeared into cab cases or into dusty piles of rough. The material that remains within the Poppy Jasper area is mostly colored a purple tinted red that works up poorly. Poppies are seldom seen.

Other nearby areas, fortunately, offer a diversity of excellent cutting rough. The community of Carefree is located north of Cave Creek, and north of Carefree, collectors can find a bold red jasper that delivers an outstanding cabochon. The material is mostly unpatterned. A few of the chunks will have the crimson interrupted by the characteristic white lines of uncolored quartz. The jasper is locally called "Ruby Rock" or "Ruby Jasper." This jasper tends to "bleed" at the grinder, but the finished product is eye-catching. Work the

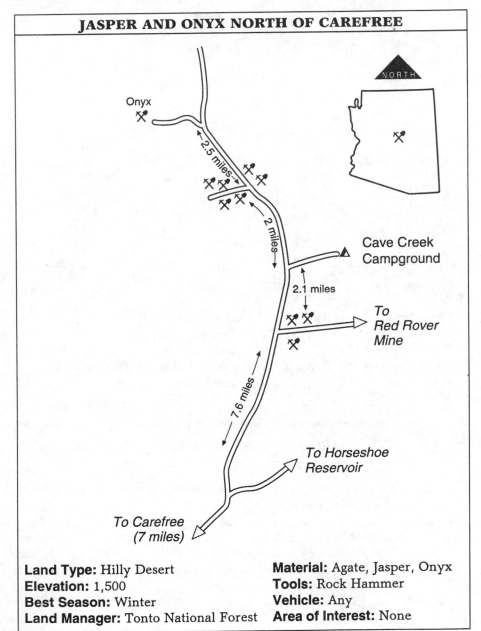

JASPER AND ONYX NORTH OF CAREFREE

Onyx

2.5 miles

2 miles

Cave Creek Campground

2.1 miles

To Red Rover Mine

7.6 miles

To Horseshoe Reservoir

To Carefree (7 miles)

NORTH

Land Type: Hilly Desert
Elevation: 1,500
Best Season: Winter
Land Manager: Tonto National Forest

Material: Agate, Jasper, Onyx
Tools: Rock Hammer
Vehicle: Any
Area of Interest: None

jasper cold and wet for best results.

An area a mile or two up the road offers jasper of a different sort. Some of this red jasper carries an interior pattern giving it the name "Spiderweb Jasper." Other pieces may have the characteristic white interruptions and other patterns.

An abandoned travertine onyx mine in the area tapped into a vein of attractive banded red, white, and brown onyx. The material is solid and will polish nearly as well as most other travertine onyx. If you are an onyx hound, don't pass by this location.

A vast area here contains a multiplicity of jasper and agate. The area is somewhat centered near the Camp Creek Campground. Much of the land between here and the Verde River (east) and Interstate 17 (west) will yield cutting rough, mostly in the form of jasper. The same can be said of the area that lies north of the well-maintained road that leads west from Cave Creek to connect with Interstate 17 at New River.

Much of the land within this area is a part of the Tonto National Forest. Don't laugh when you look at these scrubby desert hills and try to find the forest. There is a forest within the Tonto, but it is located far to the north and east of this location. A map of the Tonto forest, however, can be a fine friend to the collector. A list of national forests is found in the reference section of this book.

All of the lands described under this heading are desert and semi-desert. Summertime temperatures are not conducive to comfortable collecting. All areas are remote.

SITE 45: *CHALCEDONY AT ROUND MOUNTAIN*

The Round Mountain chalcedony deposit is at the end of a rugged road that will test the skill (and the nerves) of even experienced off-roaders. Hounds who develop a hankering to collect the Round Mountain chalcedony (some of it will contain fire) must drive from Arizona into New Mexico, back into Arizona, and then traverse a primitive BLM road that is sometimes good, sometimes bad, and sometimes *&õ#$%!

The Round Mountain chalcedony is easily found. The waxy white (sometimes brown and white) material lies in stark contrast to the darker ground color. Part of the chalcedony will be in the form that is sometimes called "desert roses." Some will incorporate the sardonyx color that can contain the fire. The most promising pieces will have the sardonyx to the bottom (the part originally attached to the host rock) with a covering of clear or slightly cloudy chalcedony. Saw or grind down through the chalcedony cap to expose the fire. Stop as soon as the fire starts to show through. This will allow you to remove a layer of "dead" material during the final sanding. If worked correctly, the fire layer will be brilliantly exposed. Go a bit too far,

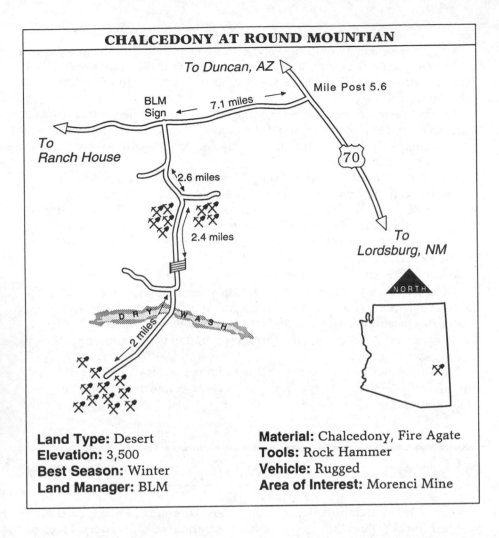

CHALCEDONY AT ROUND MOUNTIAN

To Duncan, AZ

Mile Post 5.6

BLM Sign   7.1 miles

To Ranch House

2.6 miles

2.4 miles

2 miles

DRY WASH

70

To Lordsburg, NM

NORTH

Land Type: Desert
Elevation: 3,500
Best Season: Winter
Land Manager: BLM

Material: Chalcedony, Fire Agate
Tools: Rock Hammer
Vehicle: Rugged
Area of Interest: Morenci Mine

and you risk grinding through the fire. If you do not grind far enough, the fire will be less brilliant.

The material here is truly wild chalcedony. Four-wheel-drive vehicles are recommended. Even so, practice all of the precautions recommended under the chapter titled "Desert Travel."

SITE 46: *PELONCILLO FIRE AGATE*

The chalcedony deposits located within the foothills of the rugged Peloncillo Mountain Range has been a popular rockhound destination for decades. The Bureau of Land Management has responded to that interest, and the area of the agate has been designated as The Black Hills Rockhound Area, one of the very few such areas in Arizona and one of the few nationwide. The designation protects the public nature of the area, maintaining access for all.

The area within Black Hills Rockhound Area is generously endowed with chalcedony. Most of it is the typical snow white. Some of the pieces combine snow white chalcedony and glassy chalcedony. Part of the latter shows the characteristic chalcedony "clouds." A very small part of the chalcedony here shows a varying brown color band. Pieces with the dark sardonyx color banding sometimes hold fire. The best of the fire agate from this deposit shows a bold red primary fire with exciting green flashes. Color can range from red to orange to yellow to green. Even the chalcedony that holds no fire, it should be mentioned, can be cut into handsome cabochons. This is particularly true of the chalcedony that has some shade of brown associated with the white and the clear.

The land near the registration area is the heaviest hit because it is the most accessible. Hounds who walk a ways and hunt the hills away from the road will find the best material. A number of chalcedony seams grace the hills. Hounds who have the proclivity to dig will often be well rewarded. The name Peloncillo (say Pay-lon-see-oh) is Spanish for sugar loaf. One peak within the range resembled a sugar loaf and the name Peloncillo eventually came to designate the entire range. The road to the rockhound area is well-main-

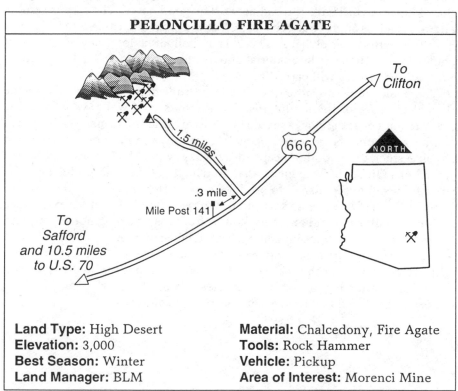

PELONCILLO FIRE AGATE

To Clifton

1.5 miles

666

NORTH

.3 mile

Mile Post 141

To Safford and 10.5 miles to U.S. 70

Land Type: High Desert
Elevation: 3,000
Best Season: Winter
Land Manager: BLM

Material: Chalcedony, Fire Agate
Tools: Rock Hammer
Vehicle: Pickup
Area of Interest: Morenci Mine

tained. Passenger cars can make the traverse if the driver exercises common sense.

The Peloncillo fire site can become uncomfortably hot during the middle of the summer. Winter temperatures will vary. Some of the peaks within the range are more than a mile high and that can cause them to blow a cold wind upon the flats. The most comfortable collecting time, generally, are the transitional seasons of spring and fall. The U.S. Geological Survey map prepared for the Silver City, New Mexico/Arizona area (1954, revised 1970) can be a navigational help in finding your way to the Peloncillo fire and to other collecting sites within the area covered.

SITE 47: *CHALCEDONY NEAR WHITLOCK MOUNTAINS*

A brown and white chalcedony can be found near the south end of the Whitlock Mountains. The Whitlocks are a short but rugged range that accents the northern end of the sprawling San Simon (say San See-moan) Valley. The Whitlock Mountain site was at one time designated a rockhound area by the Bureau of Land Management. Budget considerations (maintaining the many miles of road was expensive) caused a cancellation. The area is remote and the road is rough. That's the bad news. The good news? The area is remote and the road is rough, thus causing all but the most determined to turn their hounding efforts elsewhere. There is a hell of a lot (maybe more) of chalcedony. Much of the material shows the sardonyx color band. Some browns and whites will carry fire.

The chalcedony is scattered over a large collecting area that follows the flats at the base of the mountains. Rockhounds who walk away from the roads to hunt near the slopes should be well rewarded. The material is typical southern Arizona chalcedony, a chocolate sardonyx band (some with the host rhyolite stuck to the bottom) capped by waxy white chalcedony. Attractive cabochons can be cut from pieces that hold no fire. Often pieces that hold the fire can be cut and polished to produce superb stones.

Take Central Avenue north from downtown Bowie for about two miles and turn right (east) on Fan Road. Watch for a road turning north (left) and follow that road to a pumping station. The detailed map that accompanies the text will provide further directions. The remote aspect of the site, coupled with the roughness of the road, limits this site to hounds who drive pickup trucks and other high-clearance vehicles. Four-wheel drive may not be necessary but would add a measure of mental comfort.

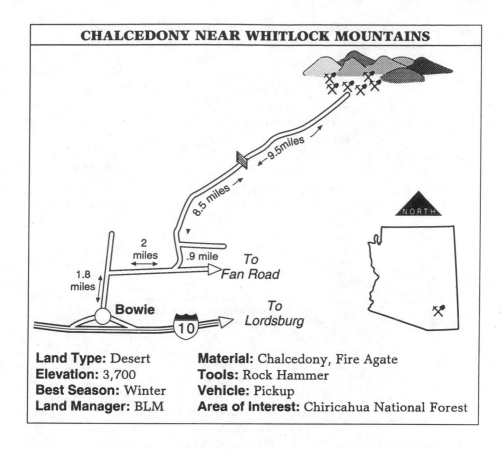

CHALCEDONY NEAR WHITLOCK MOUNTAINS

9.5miles

8.5 miles

NORTH

2 miles

.9 mile

To Fan Road

1.8 miles

Bowie

10

To Lordsburg

Land Type: Desert
Elevation: 3,700
Best Season: Winter
Land Manager: BLM

Material: Chalcedony, Fire Agate
Tools: Rock Hammer
Vehicle: Pickup
Area of Interest: Chiricahua National Forest

SITE 48: *SELENITE NEAR ST. DAVID*

Selenite (a variety of gypsum) crystal clusters can be found south and east of the southern Arizona town of St. David. The area is accessible to about any type of vehicle if the collector is willing to walk the last mile or so. Pickup trucks or vehicles equipped with four-wheel drive should be able to drive the last mile of rugged road without problems.

The selenite found in the low and flat-topped hills of the collecting area is typical of selenite found within other deposits. Surface material will be weathered. The clusters dug from the loosely compacted soil will be sharp but will be exceedingly fragile. Although it has not been established as fact, it is likely that the deposit here regenerates with rainfall, in somewhat the same way the well-known selenite deposits near Jet, Oklahoma, regenerate.

Collect along the slopes of the hills. Watch red-brown areas, as these seem to be most productive. A hand trowel will be an effective tool. The fragility of the clusters as they are exposed to the air makes the use of more efficient tools inadvisable. The crystal clusters are locally called selenite roses because some clusters bear a superficial resemblance to that flower. Some locals will tell you (with a straight face) that the clusters are petrified roses. In actuality the roseate form is one of the many fascinating forms of selenite crystallization.

Transporting fragile and semi-fragile specimens can be a problem. Some collectors have found empty egg cartons to be a sensible container. Individual clusters (after drying) can be placed within the egg holders. Most will survive the trip to the truck and the trip home.

To reach the area take the Benson exit from Interstate 10 and travel seven miles, or until you see the buildings of the Apache Powder Plant to your right. Continue on for about one-half mile. You will see a rutty road (locally called an Arizona Freeway) to your right. If your vehicle has the muscle to do so, follow this road for about a mile until you reach the flat-topped hills.

The selenite clusters can be found within a surprisingly generous area. Walking back into the hills might offer the opportunity to collect larger and more perfect specimens. Collectors who are sharp-eyed will discover other interesting crystallizations within the formation. An interesting banded rhyolite is also present.

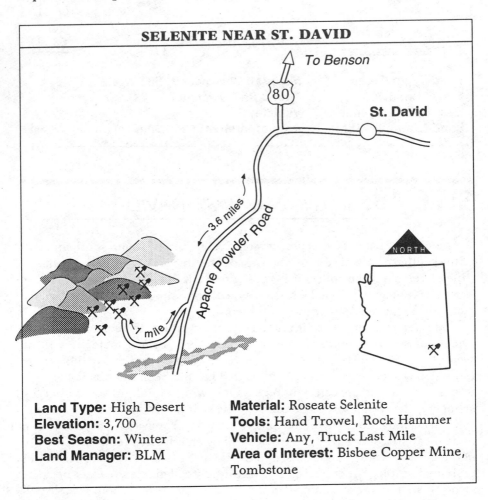

SELENITE NEAR ST. DAVID

Land Type: High Desert
Elevation: 3,700
Best Season: Winter
Land Manager: BLM

Material: Roseate Selenite
Tools: Hand Trowel, Rock Hammer
Vehicle: Any, Truck Last Mile
Area of Interest: Bisbee Copper Mine, Tombstone

The St. David selenite is fragile when first dug and must be handled gently.

SITE 49: *MYSTERY PLUME OF THE CORONADOS*

Lost gold mines and lost treasures are somewhat common to the West. Fact and fiction often cooperate to produce a colorful legend that has endured the passage of time. Lost agate deposits, although less common, do exist. One such is the instance of spectacular plume agate supposedly found within the rough country at the extreme southeast corner of Arizona.

The rough, according to an article printed in the November 1963 issue of *Lapidary Journal* was found by a man who lacked knowledge of lapidary subjects. Why he bothered to collect this particular piece was not explained. A few months later he took the rock to a Phoenix shop. Slabbing revealed a clear agate interior decorated by a single yellow plume. Other areas contained a pleasing green moss. The rockshop proprietor was able to cut three handsome cabs from the small chunk of rough. Excited, the proprietor made several trips to the reported site of discovery. He found agate, some containing plume, but none to compare with the beautiful piece delivered to his shop.

Does a gorgeous plume agate hide out in the corner of Arizona bordered by New Mexico to the east and Old Mexico to the South? Maybe. Some knowledgeable lapidaries have examined the "Coronado Plume" and have commented that it is identical in appearance to some of the plume found at the old Priday Ranch in Oregon. Even so, it is pleasant to ponder the possibility of a high quality plume deposit hidden out within a remote section of Arizona. A hard working rockhound, one day, may stumble upon this lost rock of the Coronados.

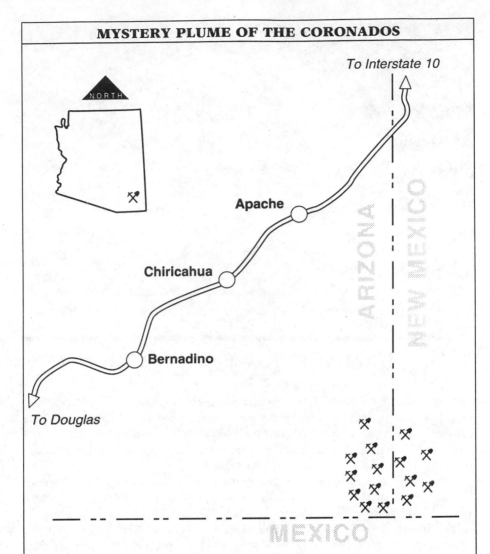

MYSTERY PLUME OF THE CORONADOS

To Interstate 10

NORTH

Apache

Chiricahua

Bernadino

To Douglas

ARIZONA

NEW MEXICO

MEXICO

Land Type: Desert
Elevation: 4,000
Best Season: Summer, Fall
Land Manager: BLM

Material: Plume Agate
Tools: ???????
Vehicle: ??????
Area of Interest: Coronado National Forest

SITE 50: *TURQUOISE EAST OF MORRISTOWN*

The area to the east of the wide place in the road called Morristown is pocked with prospects. Part of those many prospects have given up the jewelry rock turquoise. Morristown lapidary Martin Koning (who has a rock shop there) reports that he has collected turquoise from an abandoned prospect near the Maricopa/Yavapai county line on the Castle Hot Springs Road. The county line is located about fourteen miles east of the road's junction with U.S. 60 at Morristown. Early miners, Martin says, ran a drift into the side of the mountain searching for profitable ore. The turquoise vein was exposed and a few specks remain.

Martin worked hard all afternoon and ended up with a double handful of hard blue vein material and nuggets. Taking the turquoise from the half-inch vein that cuts the ironstone is hard work for small reward. Hard rock mining tools, perspiration (and at times, strong language), are required.

Rock writer Bob Jones, in an article printed in the September 1975 issue

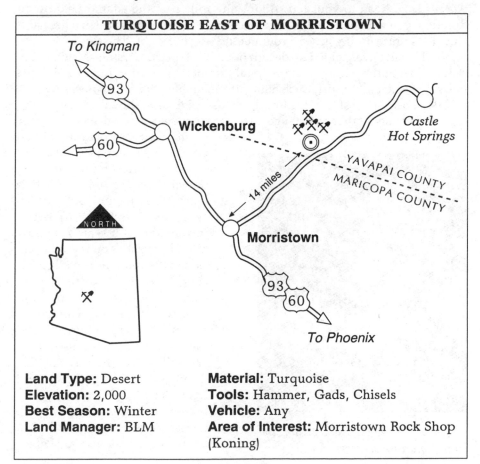

TURQUOISE EAST OF MORRISTOWN

To Kingman

Wickenburg

Castle Hot Springs

YAVAPAI COUNTY
MARICOPA COUNTY

14 miles

NORTH

Morristown

To Phoenix

Land Type: Desert
Elevation: 2,000
Best Season: Winter
Land Manager: BLM

Material: Turquoise
Tools: Hammer, Gads, Chisels
Vehicle: Any
Area of Interest: Morristown Rock Shop (Koning)

of *Rock and Gem Magazine*, reports a turquoise location within the same area. Although he is not specific about location, it is likely that the half-inch wide turquoise seam he focuses on in the article is in the same area.

This second turquoise location, as described in the article, yields a soft and semi-soft kind of turquoise that must be treated to be suitable for jewelry use. The material, according to Jones, was somewhat plentiful.

It is likely that other prospects within this highly mineralized area carry some turquoise. A diligent search might turn up additional occurrences.

SITE 51: *QUARTZ CRYSTALS AT DATE CREEK*

The Date Creek collecting area is another hard-hit area. Easy accessibility, pleasant winter temperatures, and adequate parking for RVs mean that hills and washes here are frequently visited. To reach the area, drive north from Wickenberg on U.S. 93 for about twenty-three miles. Watch for the dirt Alamo Lake Road to your left. About one mile past the Alamo Lake Road junction, you will see a well-maintained dirt road to your right. Turn here and travel 1.8 miles until you see a rounded hill to your right. The slopes and the top of this hill have yielded up decent pockets of quartz crystals. Much of the material from this hill is cluster crystals stained brown by limonite. Keep a bucket of water and a stiff brush handy to clean the specimens for evaluation.

The most successful collectors here use pick and shovel to locate the crystal pockets and then change to a long-handled screwdriver or other

Some Date Creek crystals exhibit the somewhat rare scepter habit.

prying device to isolate individual crystals or clusters. Do not spend all of your time on the hill. Even though evidence will suggest that most of the digging activity occurs here, you will be better rewarded if you search the low hills and washes on the opposite side of the road. Knowledgeable collectors time their trip here to coincide with the end of summer, sometime after October 1. A series of hard summer rains, the kind locals call gully washers, will scour the dirt and the diggings to clean and expose a fresh crop of crystals. Sometimes these across-the-road crystals will demonstrate the scepter habit. Some are pleasingly large, perhaps six inches long with a termination that may be an inch or more in diameter.

Few of the Date Creek crystals will be clear enough to facet. Crystals collected here will serve mainly as specimen pieces, as "candy for the eyes." Collectors who have an interest and a belief in the metaphysical quality of quartz will find many interesting examples. The Date Creek quartz singles look mighty fetching as a dangle for the shirt or pendant for the neck.

If your visit is timed for summer's end, drive on down Date Creek Road to the Date Creek Ranch. Phil Knight maintains an apple and a peach orchard, protected by the walls of Date Creek Canyon and nourished with water from Date Creek itself. Mr. Knight allows fee collecting of the fruit (mostly on weekends) during the season.

The road, for all practical purposes, ends at the ranch. Those who own four-wheel-drive vehicles (and nerves of steel) can sometimes ford the creek to connect with a primitive two track that leads into the Date Creek Mountains. It is not a trip you will enjoy.

QUARTZ CRYSTALS AT DATE CREEK

Land Type: Desert	**Material:** Quartz Crystals
Elevation: 2,200	**Tools:** Gads, Chisels, Hammer
Best Season: Winter	**Vehicle:** Any
Land Manager: BLM	**Area of Interest:** Alamo Lake State Park

SITE 52: *CHALCEDONY AT BLACK MOUNTAIN*

Interesting chunks of waxy white chalcedony can be found on the flats and the west-facing slopes of Black Mountain. Black Mountain is black and is of somewhat recent volcanic origin. The waxy white of the chalcedony (at times called "desert roses") makes them obvious even to the inexperienced eye.

The Black Mountain chalcedony deposit has been a popular collecting area for decades. Even so, each rain exposes new material. The areas most accessible have been hardest hit. Collectors willing to walk a bit are likely to find the best pickings.

The Black Mountain area is typical Arizona desert—flat land covered with greasewood (creosote bush), low ridges graced by that odd member of the lily family called the Joshua Tree, washes that are wet only during runoff, stark mountains composed mostly of recent volcanic rock—inhospitable country

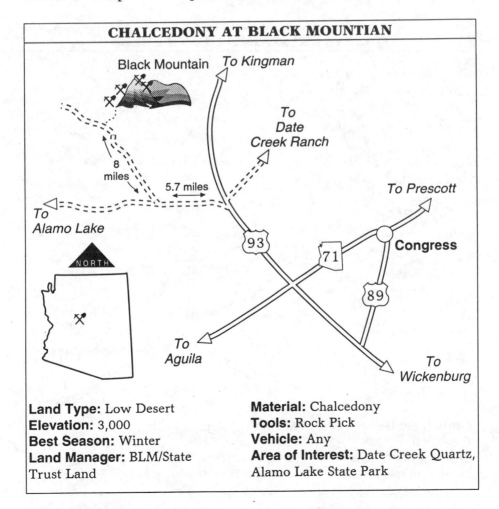

CHALCEDONY AT BLACK MOUNTIAN

Black Mountain — To Kingman

To Date Creek Ranch

8 miles

5.7 miles

To Alamo Lake

To Prescott

93

71

Congress

89

NORTH

To Aguila

To Wickenburg

Land Type: Low Desert
Elevation: 3,000
Best Season: Winter
Land Manager: BLM/State Trust Land

Material: Chalcedony
Tools: Rock Pick
Vehicle: Any
Area of Interest: Date Creek Quartz, Alamo Lake State Park

during the summer months of June, July, August, and September.

Winter temperatures can be great. The desert is occupied mostly by the coyote (you will hear their singing at night), the desert mule deer, an occasional desert bighorn sheep, and a multitude of smaller animals, most active only at night. The nearby Date Creek quartz crystal deposit allows an opportunity to collect a diversification of material.

Those who visit here in April will have an opportunity to view the spectacular blooming of several species of cacti. The hedgehog can be particularly attractive, presenting a fuschia bloom as big as a fair-sized fist. Spineless varieties of prickly pear also present the fuschia flower. The ordinary variety of prickly pear becomes covered with a bright yellow blossom.

The spring weather that brings blossoms can also bring snakes. The warming weather of March and April encourages rattlesnakes to abandon hibernation. Be alert, particularly around rocky areas, at this time of year. The large-bodied western diamondback and the smaller but more deadly Mohave are the common types.

SITE 53: *OBSIDIAN AT BURRO CREEK*

The obsidian nodules found near the Burro Creek Bridge on U.S. 93 are unremarkable. Most are small (marble-sized) and all own a common dull exterior. The interior of the "tears" is mostly of two types. One type is opaque. The second contains an attractive banding, some a smoky color with alternating bands nearly black. A trip through the tumbler will allow identification. Some of the banded nodules, properly oriented, will deliver up an attractive "cat's eye" stone.

Even the opaque variety of obsidian has a lapidary use. Some crafters cut thin slices to use as a backing to construct an opal doublet. Others cut slices to use as a substitute for jet when constructing inlay jewelry.

Keep the sun to your back as you collect the obsidian. A low sun, early morning or late afternoon, can be helpful. Walk slowly and keep a sharp eye working to discover these charcoal look-alikes. Some obsidian can be found on the flat area to the southeast of the BLM campground located on the south bank of Burro Creek, although this easily accessible area is the hardest hit and is likely to be the least productive. Other tears can be found by crossing the fence south of the campground (a metal gate is close by) to hunt the bluffs a short hike across the fence. Other tears can be found on the north side of the creek (water flow is intermittent and the creek bed is sometimes completely dry). If you are physically fit and feel frisky, you can hike up the canyon formed by Burro Creek a mile or more where excellent jasper can be found.

For specific directions, consult the directions that follow, under the heading "Patterned Jasper Near Burro Creek Bridge."

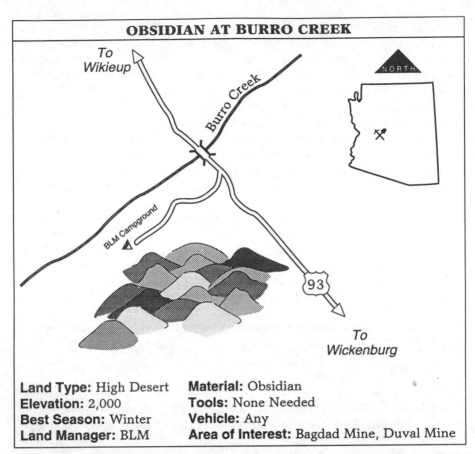

OBSIDIAN AT BURRO CREEK

To Wikieup

Burro Creek

NORTH

BLM Campground

93

To Wickenburg

Land Type: High Desert
Elevation: 2,000
Best Season: Winter
Land Manager: BLM

Material: Obsidian
Tools: None Needed
Vehicle: Any
Area of Interest: Bagdad Mine, Duval Mine

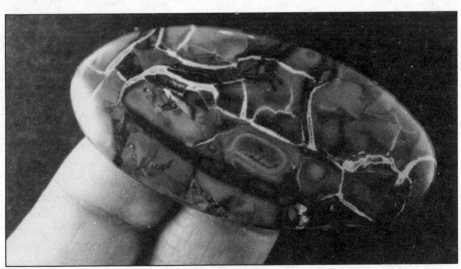

This cabochon of "Sugar Loaf Mountain" jasper contains brown, red, and white in a pleasing combination.

SITE 54: *PATTERNED JASPER NEAR BURRO CREEK BRIDGE*

A deposit of attractive patterned jasper is located a mile or two northeast of the Burro Creek Bridge on U.S. 93. Even though the author visited the site twenty-five years ago, his memory of that wild ride remains bright. Super rockhound Lou Long of Wikieup was at the wheel. Lou followed two track roads, no-track washes, and even did a good bit of cross-country travel to take us close to the distinctive desert hill that produced the jasper.

The material was scattered among the low hills and flats that joined the southeast facing slope of the mountain. Jasper chunks ranged from egg size (AA extra large) to a size too heavy to lift. The base color of the jasper is a pleasant brown. The patterns can be a deeper brown, white, or red. One piece collected there was slabbed to show a series of druse-filled vugs and a bold red pattern.

Could a motivated person four-wheel his way close to the deposit? I couldn't. That same strange mountain, however, can be seen by a hound who

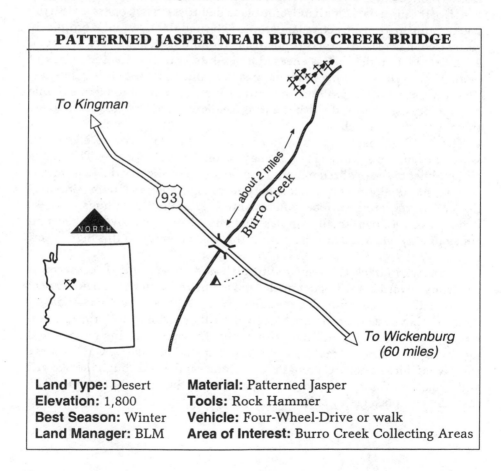

PATTERNED JASPER NEAR BURRO CREEK BRIDGE

To Kingman

93

NORTH

about 2 miles

Burro Creek

To Wickenburg
(60 miles)

Land Type: Desert   **Material:** Patterned Jasper
Elevation: 1,800   **Tools:** Rock Hammer
Best Season: Winter   **Vehicle:** Four-Wheel-Drive or walk
Land Manager: BLM   **Area of Interest:** Burro Creek Collecting Areas

looks upstream (northeast) from the Burro Creek Bridge. A long, tough hike will take him or her to the collecting area. Considering the distance in, the distance out, and the ruggedness of the terrain, a collector who made the march would find it necessary to be very, very selective.

The same remote ridge that makes the jasper, the author suspects, likely produces a variety of other gem rough.

The jasper from this location is hard and usually offers no difficulty in the cutting and the cabbing. Work just as you would other jaspers. Grind through the 320 wheel (if your unit has one) or through the 220 wheel. Sand wet on 180 through a used 600 grit. Finish on leather or canvas saturated with tin or cerium oxide.

SITE 55: *DENDRITIC OPAL AT BURRO CREEK*

This common opal is actually an opal replacement of bentonite. The background color is a yellow-brown or red and is translucent in thin slices. Much of the material holds handsome black dendrites that cooperate with the background to form attractive landscapes. The nodular material is ordinarily recovered in fist-sized chunks (small fists, medium fists, large fists, and even XXL fists.) Often the rock is encased in a white or cream-colored casing of opal. That exterior coating is sometimes liberally endowed with dendrites. The thin aspect of the white cover, and its nature, cause it to be unsuitable for lapidary use. It is the dendrite bearing a yellow or red interior that delivers the outstanding cabochons.

The opalized bentonite (a bedded plastic-like clay that swells when wetted) occurs in a white clay that may be unaltered bentonite. The seams and nodules of the opalized material can be found by digging down a yard or so into the unaltered clay. Look for the prospect holes left by previous diggers. If you are a surface collector only, examine the tailings of these diggings to discover small samples that may have been overlooked and subsequently washed by the hard rains that infrequently hit this high desert area.

Those who attack the seams with pick and shovel will reap the most generous reward here. The dendritic opal is a prized material. Do not expect to fill a truck bed with the material. Hundreds (maybe thousands) of collectors have been here before you. Even so, those willing to work, and who have rockhound luck, can leave with booty. The opalite is fine-grained and mostly without flaws. Treat it as you would any other silicate. Cut the slabs somewhat thick to ensure strength. Grind and sand wet through the 600 grit and polish on leather or canvas slopped with tin or cerium oxide. The material accepts a glassy shine.

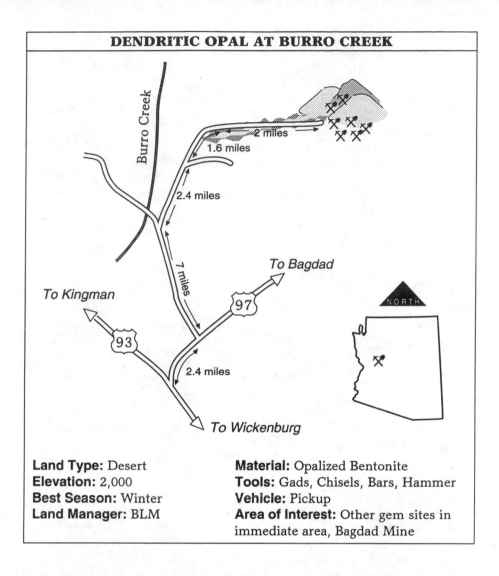

DENDRITIC OPAL AT BURRO CREEK

Burro Creek

2 miles

1.6 miles

2.4 miles

To Bagdad

To Kingman

7 miles

97

93

2.4 miles

To Wickenburg

NORTH

Land Type: Desert
Elevation: 2,000
Best Season: Winter
Land Manager: BLM

Material: Opalized Bentonite
Tools: Gads, Chisels, Bars, Hammer
Vehicle: Pickup
Area of Interest: Other gem sites in immediate area, Bagdad Mine

SITE 56: *PASTELITE ALONG BURRO CREEK*

Tons of attractive pastelite have been removed from this prolific collecting site. Tons of material remain. Much of the material is available as float, some of it in boulders too large to load. More material is underground, in seams, available to those who like to dig. Diggers should come equipped with the usual assortment of agony sticks—picks, shovels, hammers, and gads—along with leather gloves and eye protectors.

The main color of the pastelite is creamy to flesh pink. A good bit of the material is swirled with contrasting colors, almost always subdued pastels of brown, orange, red, and tan. The Burro Creek pastelite is nearly always solid and is fine-grained. Obtaining a glassy polish is a matter of careful sanding followed by buffing on leather or canvas slopped with tin or cerium oxide.

Army officers from Camp Tollgate visited the area in 1869 and named the desert stream Burro Creek. It is likely they saw burros in the area and were thus inspired. Prospectors who starved out, or who were attacked by Indians, commonly turned their burros loose so that they could live off the land. The descendants of those burros can be seen within the area to this day. In some areas they have reproduced to the point that the habitat can no longer support them. Many are corralled by BLM employees and offered out for adoption.

Summer collecting can be uncomfortably warm. Summer collectors, almost always, limit collecting to the cooler, early morning hours. An attractive campground sits a short distance south of the pastelite deposit.

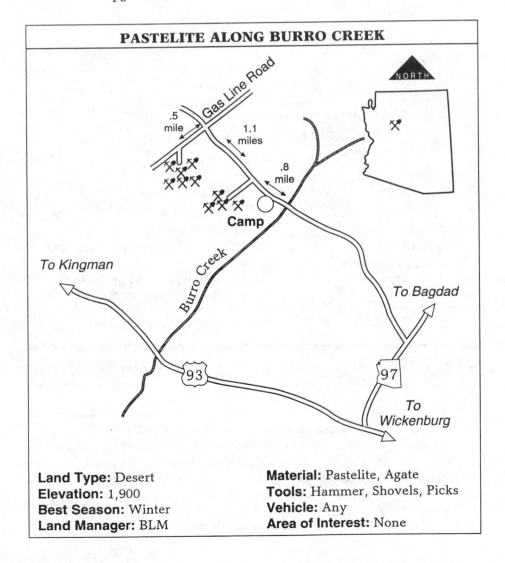

PASTELITE ALONG BURRO CREEK

Land Type: Desert
Elevation: 1,900
Best Season: Winter
Land Manager: BLM

Material: Pastelite, Agate
Tools: Hammer, Shovels, Picks
Vehicle: Any
Area of Interest: None

SITE 57: *COPPER MINERALS NEAR AGUILA*

The Harcuvar Mountain Range can be seen by looking north from the town of Aguila. A well-maintained dirt road leads from Aguila to the top of Pete Smith Peak, a mountain readily recognizable by the profusion of towers on top. A mile or two before the road begins to climb the Harcuvars (an Indian word meaning "little water," certainly true), a rougher road angles to the right (east). This somewhat rugged road leads to a series of copper prospects located within obvious red ryolite hills that decorate the otherwise flat desert. About two miles in, the road reaches a flat. A rusty grizzly decorates part of

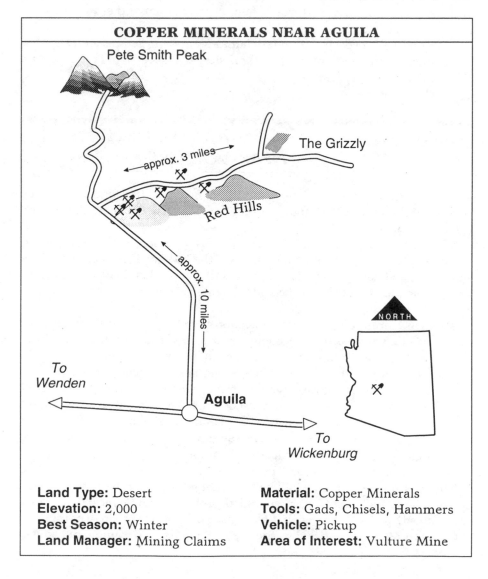

COPPER MINERALS NEAR AGUILA

Pete Smith Peak

The Grizzly

approx. 3 miles

Red Hills

approx. 10 miles

To Wenden

NORTH

Aguila

To Wickenburg

Land Type: Desert
Elevation: 2,000
Best Season: Winter
Land Manager: Mining Claims

Material: Copper Minerals
Tools: Gads, Chisels, Hammers
Vehicle: Pickup
Area of Interest: Vulture Mine

that flat, and in front of the grizzly is a booty pile of fist-sized rhyolite seamed with a variety of copper ores. Chrysocolla and malachite are the most obvious. Red within the blue and green suggests the presence of cuprite. The black of tenorite peeks through occasionally.

The dumps of surrounding prospects offer similar material. The rock is mostly specimen material only. The multicolored seams are thin. A few, with careful sawing, will yield up a seam thick enough to cut if a backing of rhyolite is left to provide strength.

An in situ seam of the copper ore is available at one prospect. As you approach the area on the Smith Peak Road, while turning to the right to take the road that leads to the prospects, look to your right and you will see the point of a rhyolite hill. The seam is on the north-facing side of that point. You will need gads, chisels, and heavy hammers to remove the ore from the stubborn rhyolite.

Many of the prospects are under claim and are worked periodically. Do not disturb equipment you may find on site. **Respect "No Trespassing" signs that may be present.**

SITE 58: *OBSIDIAN NODULES NEAR VULTURE MINE*

A generous scattering of small obsidian nodules, the kind sometimes called Apache Tears, can be found upon a flat located between Aguila and the carcass of the Vulture Mine.

The exterior of these marble-sized blobs is weathered and uninspiring. They look like lumps of dull charcoal. But the interior is interesting. Some show a silky sheen when polished (tumbled). Those that do can be taken to the combination unit to be worked into the interesting cabochons called cat's eyes.

The same area offers snowy chalcedony, some showing the white-on-white banding typical of chalcedony, and a few showing the handsome cordovan banding (sardonyx) that sometimes contains fire. None of the chalcedony here, to the author's knowledge, has produced fire agate.

The nearby Vulture Mine, now inactive, was once the premiere gold property in Arizona (eventually exceeded by The Congress, the United Eastern, and other mines within Mohave County). The mine was "dry," the nearest water source being the Hassayampa River twelve miles east. Wickenburg showed sense when he sold the unprocessed ore for $15 per ton to miners who used arrastras to work out the gold.

The Vulture gave up $2.5 million worth of gold during the first six years of operation. Much more was high-graded (stolen) by employees. It has been speculated that a German, Jacob Walz, was in cahoots with a thief, or thieves, at the Vulture, taking the high-grade ore to Phoenix by a roundabout route,

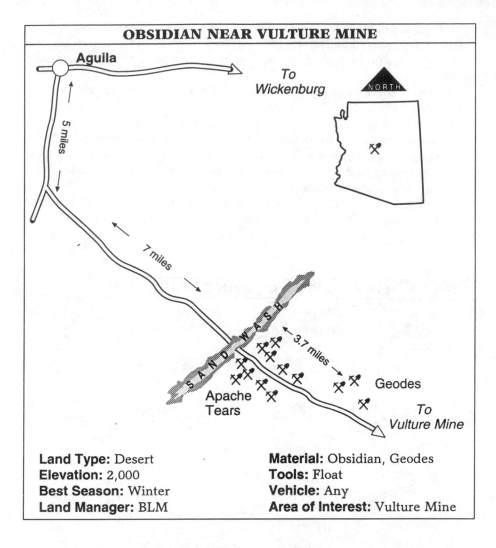

OBSIDIAN NEAR VULTURE MINE

Aguila

To Wickenburg

NORTH

5 miles

7 miles

SAND WASH

3.7 miles

Apache Tears

Geodes

To Vulture Mine

Land Type: Desert
Elevation: 2,000
Best Season: Winter
Land Manager: BLM

Material: Obsidian, Geodes
Tools: Float
Vehicle: Any
Area of Interest: Vulture Mine

saying it came from his "Lost Dutchman Mine" within the Superstition Mountains.

Even though the Vulture Mine is now inactive, and has been for many years, an interesting museum is located on site. An admittance fee is charged.

SITE 59: *FIRE AGATE AT SADDLE MOUNTAIN*

The slopes of Saddle Mountain have been hit and hit hard. Fifty years of frantic collecting by amateur and commercial collectors has caused nearly every piece of brown-banded float to disappear. Persistent collectors have climbed the mountain to wrest in situ chalcedony from the tough granite.

But quality material remains. Each new rain, it seems, exposes fresh material. Sharp-eyed collectors, those willing to work slowly, keep the sun to their back, and look sharply, can come away with a handful of quality rough.

Not every piece of waxy white chalcedony found here will contain the brown banding (sardonyx) that contains the fire. Not every piece of white and brown chalcedony will contain fire. Even so, every piece of the chalcedony holds gemstone value. Even the pure white pieces sometimes contain an interesting design. Even the fireless brown and whites can be cut to show interesting patterns. And like chalcedony everywhere, the Saddle Mountain material accepts an excellent polish.

Experienced chalcedony collectors know that the little critters can hide out in the strangest places. Collecting early and late in the day, when the sun is low, can be particularly rewarding. Watch carefully for a tiny touch of

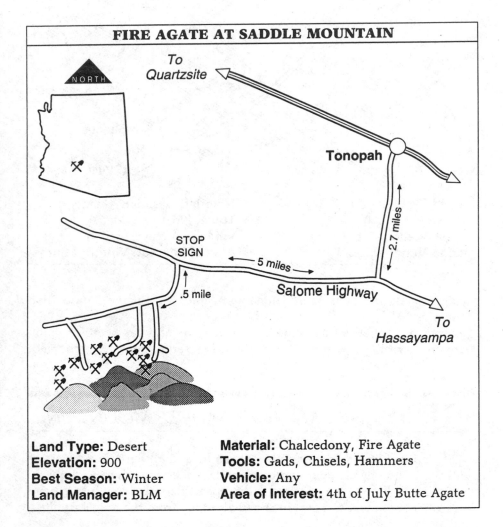

FIRE AGATE AT SADDLE MOUNTAIN

To Quartzsite

NORTH

Tonopah

2.7 miles

STOP SIGN

← 5 miles →

.5 mile

Salome Highway

To Hassayampa

Land Type: Desert
Elevation: 900
Best Season: Winter
Land Manager: BLM

Material: Chalcedony, Fire Agate
Tools: Gads, Chisels, Hammers
Vehicle: Any
Area of Interest: 4th of July Butte Agate

white. Investigation might reveal the "tip of the iceberg." A choice specimen might be peeking through, awaiting liberation.

Search the base of the mountain (the west side will be most productive) and as far up the slopes as your health and your grit will allow. Be alert for small geodes, about the size of a small, dirty peewee hen's egg. These are often crystal-filled and make attractive specimens when cut.

The fire within the Saddle Mountain chalcedony is almost always hidden away in the sardonyx. Smart collectors resist the temptation to hammer the piece to discover the beauty (or the ugly) within. Chipping can cause the piece to internally fracture. Maintain self-control and use the trim saw to uncover the fire.

Some Saddle Mountain specimens show visible fire. Working the piece to take best advantage of the fire is thus simplified. Specimens that show no surface fire can be more difficult. Take the booty to a bucket of warm soapy water. Use a scrub brush to clean away dirt and debris. Inspect the piece under bright light to seek out a clue to the fire band. If you see none, take the piece to the trim saw and saw away the white cap just above the sardonyx layer. Use the grinder, wet, to abrade away the last bit of white capping. Grind, inspecting frequently, until you see the first flash of fire. Mark out the cabochon and finish in the usual manner, doing the final polish on canvas or leather with tin or oxide.

SITE 60: FORTIFICATION AGATE AT 4TH OF JULY BUTTE

History tells us that a group traveled to this area to celebrate our country's independence and decided it was appropriate to name the dry wash where they camped to honor the occasion. A nearby butte took the same name.

The agate found among the flats of this vast collecting area is mostly float. Collectors roam the flats, keeping a watchful eye alert for the touch of white that denotes agate. The pieces are mostly small and a percentage of the area has been hit hard for dozens of years. Even so, the area continues to produce. The product is mainly a white-rimmed nodule containing swirls and bands of gray, shading to blue—a fortification agate that is hard, fracture free, and eye-catching. Some collectors here watch for dirt piles that denote recent digging. A hound who digs here sometimes will be rewarded with fist-sized nodules of the fancy fortification.

Other material is sometimes found. The author added one piece to his collection that contains a lacy white fortification pattern and a center fortification of cardinal red. Another tube-shaped nodule shows fortifications of royal purple. Red, grey, brown, and blue-gray moss agate are sometimes found.

To reach the Fourth of July area, follow Interstate 10 west from Phoenix to its junction with Arizona 85. Turn south (left) and go four miles to Palo Verde junction. Turn west and travel southwest through Palo Verde to the Arlington cattle pens. Turn west (right) at the cattle pens to travel on the Agua Caliente Road. Follow this maintained dirt road for a bit more than fourteen miles. Turn right on a set of tire tracks leading to the right. Within a half mile or so, you will see the ruins of an ancient chimney. Look for evidence of digging, as this is the site of the famous Chimney Beds. Return to Agua Caliente Road and head west.

Agate can be found on both sides of the road all the way to the butte, a distance of about seven miles. Do not neglect Fourth of July Butte as a collecting site. The slopes of this low desert mountain yield up agate and quartz crystals (mostly within geodes). Some collectors have reported finding the small lumps of obsidian, locally called Apache Tears.

Work the fortification agate just as you would any other agate. Proceed through the grinding grits, the sanding grits, and finish off with tin or cerium oxide on leather or canvas.

Winter collecting can be pleasant at the Fourth of July Butte site. Summer collecting can be uncomfortably hot and can be dangerous. Avoid the area between about May 15 and September 30.

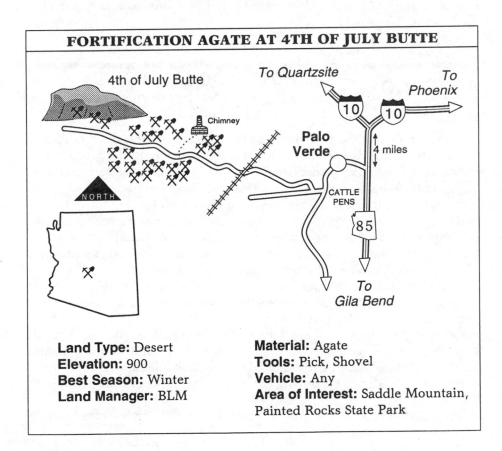

FORTIFICATION AGATE AT 4TH OF JULY BUTTE

4th of July Butte

To Quartzsite

To Phoenix

10 10

Chimney

Palo Verde

4 miles

NORTH

CATTLE PENS

85

To Gila Bend

Land Type: Desert
Elevation: 900
Best Season: Winter
Land Manager: BLM

Material: Agate
Tools: Pick, Shovel
Vehicle: Any
Area of Interest: Saddle Mountain, Painted Rocks State Park

Fortification agate from the Chimney Beds is generally blue with white fortification lines.

SITE 61: *PAINTED ROCK AGATE*

The south-facing slopes of the Painted Rock Mountains have been a stingy, but steady, producer of agate for many years. Many collectors stop here to stoop a bit as they travel to the jumble of petroglyphs at Painted Rock State Park, or as they travel to the Rowley Mine dumps.

The agate colors are somewhat faded; an artists palette of pastels. A few of the chunks will carry mossy inclusions.

As with most public collecting areas, the ground closest to the road has been picked nearly clean. A walk away from the road can increase collecting potential. Do your picking sensibly. Walk as far as you intend to go and collect your way back to the vehicle. Done otherwise, you will carry your booty away from the vehicle only to have to pack it back.

Agate can be found on both sides of the road. It seems to cover a substantial area and is sparsely distributed. You may need several hours to collect a substantial sample. Even so, the quality of the best material makes the search worthwhile.

The nearby Painted Rocks State Park offers an interesting variety of petroglyphs. The ancients used a sharp pointed rock (perhaps agate from the Painted Rock Mountains) to peck through the black manganese coating called desert varnish. The petroglyphs are so crowded on some rocks that it can be difficult to discern individual peckings. As with most other Arizona petroglyph

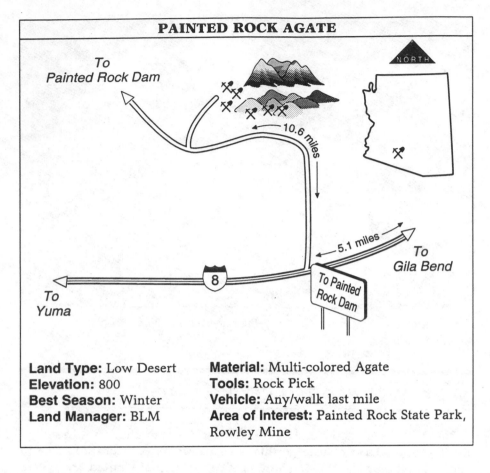

To
Painted Rock Dam

NORTH

← 10.6 miles

5.1 miles →

To
Gila Bend

8

To
Yuma

To Painted
Rock Dam

Land Type: Low Desert
Elevation: 800
Best Season: Winter
Land Manager: BLM

Material: Multi-colored Agate
Tools: Rock Pick
Vehicle: Any/walk last mile
Area of Interest: Painted Rock State Park,
Rowley Mine

locations, the peckings are a mixture of anthropomorphs and zoomorphs.

What do the peckings mean? No person now alive can answer the question correctly. But part of a petroglyphic rock, the author is almost sure, carries a straightforward message: *Good place to hunt rocks and minerals.*

SITE 62: GEMS & MINERALS IN THE EAGLE TAIL MOUNTAINS

The Eagle Tail Mountains are so named because one peak within the range, Eagle Tail Peak, resembles the tail feathers of an eagle. The area is pocked with prospects and mines. One area of the range, near Courthouse Rock, contains numerous examples of rock writing. Noted rockhound Martin Koning of Morristown once counted 2,500 petroglyphs. Martin estimates that at least 1,200 have escaped enumeration.

Many of the dumps offer the opportunity to collect copper-influenced minerals, such as bornite, chrysocolla, and malachite. Mineralized quartz stringers offer in situ minerals to those with the urge to dig. Much of the range has been incorporated into a wilderness area, closing roads. Collectors wanting to use the area must have the time and endurance needed to hike among the rugged hills.

An agate deposit is accessible on the north side of Interstate 10, and north of the Eagle Tail Mountains. Agate and chalcedony (a few pieces holding fire) can be found on a low hill about one-half mile north of the Interstate. **The Quartzsite Gem & Mineral Society has filed on the deposit to reserve the rocks for its membership. It may be necessary to join the club to be able to collect legally.**

Both the Eagle Tail Mountains and the agate area north of the Interstate are lowland desert that gets hot to the tenth power during the summer months—110 degrees in the shade, and no shade. No water. No good.

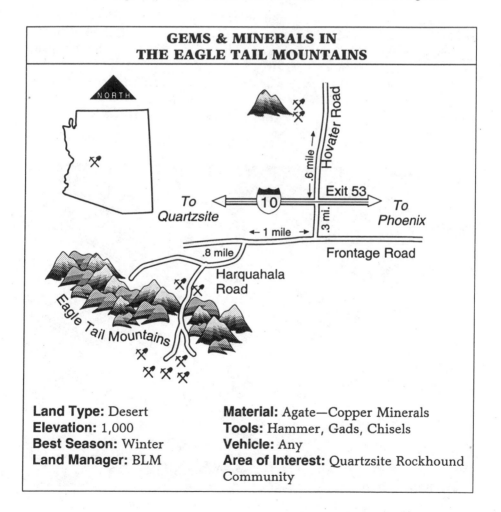

GEMS & MINERALS IN THE EAGLE TAIL MOUNTAINS

Land Type: Desert
Elevation: 1,000
Best Season: Winter
Land Manager: BLM

Material: Agate—Copper Minerals
Tools: Hammer, Gads, Chisels
Vehicle: Any
Area of Interest: Quartzsite Rockhound Community

SITE 63: *AGATE & JASPER NEAR ALAMO LAKE*

Areas near this desert lake offer a generous variety of cuttables. Cobbles of agate, jasper, and petrified wood are somewhat plentiful along ridges that overlook the Santa Maria arm of the lake. Some of the petrified wood is the variety sometimes called palm bog—the petrified remains of palm tree root. The primary color of the bog is brown. Patterns within many of the smallish pieces add interest.

The entire area surrounding the lake has gemstone potential. **All except the dedicated area within Alamo Lake State Park is open to collecting.** It is a fine place to spend some time. Camping facilities are available. Those who travel in motor homes or who tow travel trailers will find Alamo Lake State Park a pleasant place to spend a day or a week.

The lake results from the damming of the Santa Maria River. The lake outlet becomes The Bill Williams River. This typical desert impoundment is a popular destination for fishermen. The lake offers large-mouth bass, crappie, blue gill perch, and catfish.

Collectors who have access to a boat will find exploration of the coves and ridges on the north side of the lake interesting. Martin Koning reports a deposit of blue agate in rhyolite within the old copper diggings located near Ironwood Wash.

Petrified roots of ancient palm trees can be found near Lake Alamo.

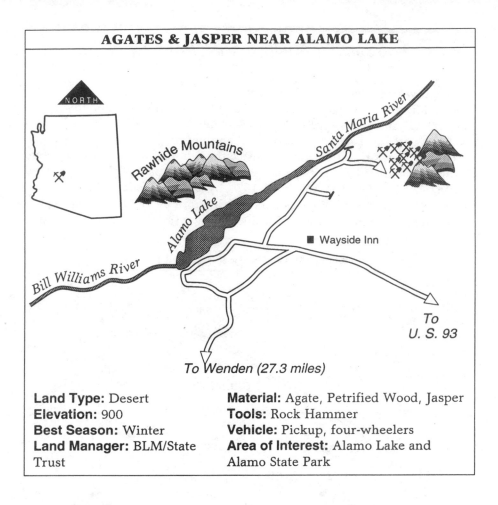

AGATES & JASPER NEAR ALAMO LAKE

NORTH

Rawhide Mountains

Santa Maria River

Alamo Lake

Bill Williams River

■ Wayside Inn

To U. S. 93

To Wenden (27.3 miles)

Land Type: Desert
Elevation: 900
Best Season: Winter
Land Manager: BLM/State Trust

Material: Agate, Petrified Wood, Jasper
Tools: Rock Hammer
Vehicle: Pickup, four-wheelers
Area of Interest: Alamo Lake and Alamo State Park

A pair of well-maintained roads leads to Alamo Lake. Access from the south is by Alamo Lake Road, which leaves U.S. 60 at Wenden and heads nearly due north through the Harcuvar Mountains at Cunningham Pass. The second access is by a graded dirt road that leaves U.S. 93 north of Congress Junction to beeline southwest to the lake. Driving time in both instances will be about one hour.

Remain particularly alert for rattlesnakes during early spring (February-March) and during early fall (October-November). The snakes are coming out of, or going into, hibernation at those times and can be particularly plentiful. The fluctuating water level of the lake can cause them to concentrate along the shoreline. The western diamondback and the Mohave are the common types.

SITE 64: *GEMSTONE & MINERALS NEAR SIGNAL*

The town of Signal was built to serve the needs of the Signal and McCrackin mines, each nine miles distant from this frontier town that hugged the bank of the Big Sandy Wash. Water from the Big Sandy supplied the town and was packed by burro to the mines.

The McCrackin and Signal mines, although separately owned, were contiguous and mined the same silver outcrop. The best of the ore assayed $600 a ton. Discovered on August 17, 1874, by Jackson McCrackin, the mines yielded more than six million dollars worth of ore by 1880. Decreasing ore value caused the mines to close. The 800 rowdy residents of Signal moved to

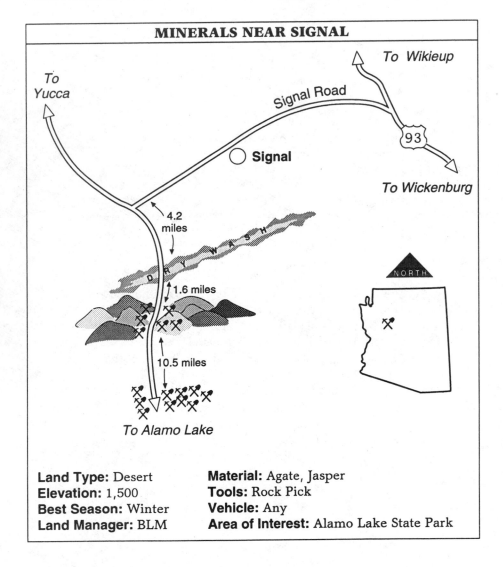

MINERALS NEAR SIGNAL

To Wikieup

To Yucca

Signal Road

93

To Wickenburg

Signal

4.2 miles

DRY WASH

NORTH

1.6 miles

10.5 miles

To Alamo Lake

Land Type: Desert
Elevation: 1,500
Best Season: Winter
Land Manager: BLM

Material: Agate, Jasper
Tools: Rock Pick
Vehicle: Any
Area of Interest: Alamo Lake State Park

more prosperous fields, and the town of Signal diminished to ghost town status.

Chert, jasper, and petrified wood can be found within a series of low hills west and south of Signal. The field is located about six miles south of the Signal Road/Alamo Lake Road junction. The gemstone seems equally plentiful on either side of the road. Gemstone size seldom exceeds fist size, about right for a ten-inch saw. Colors range from dark red to light brown.

A second collecting site is located a bit more than ten miles south. The material is dispersed over a large area and is similar to that found at the previous location. Both collecting sites are within the low country. Travel and collecting is best done during winter months. Both sites are remote. Practice all cautions listed under "Desert Travel."

SITE 65: *COPPER MINERALS AT HARQUAHALA*

The Harquahala Mine dump is extensive and hides an interesting variety of copper minerals—malachite and chrysocolla, as might be expected, but also the somewhat rare dioptase, ore specimens of pyrite and chalcopyrite, and too many more to mention. A hand lens can be helpful.

Do not expect to find much within the exposed part of the dump. Weathering and years of enthusiastic collecting have caused much of the surface material to disappear. The most successful collectors here will be the ones who earn their specimens the old fashioned way; they work for them. Heavy hammers, gads, and chisels are needed to expose seams within the gangue. Leather gloves and eye protectors are a requisite.

The Harquahala Mine was prospected by Henry Wickenburg in 1863. While making the sixty-mile march back to join the Peeples-Weaver party, ol' Henry stumbled upon the gold deposit at Vulture Peak. Actually, Henry's burro stumbled upon the deposit. The burro, according to legend, misstepped. Henry grabbed a chunk of rock and heaved it burro-ward. He missed, and the rock split, exposing rich gold. That mine was to deliver $2.5 million in gold during the next six years.

The Harquahala Mine was worked by the Bonanza Mining company between 1888 and gave up $1.6 million worth of gold during the first three years of production. The mine continued to produce gold for the next several decades but seldom at a profit to the operators.

The mine is located within the Little Harquahala Mountains, below Martin Peak. The mine is remotely situated, and the road can be rough. Summer temperatures exceed 100 degrees nearly every day between June 1 and September 30. And even though the name Harquahala means "place of the water," do not count on finding water close by.

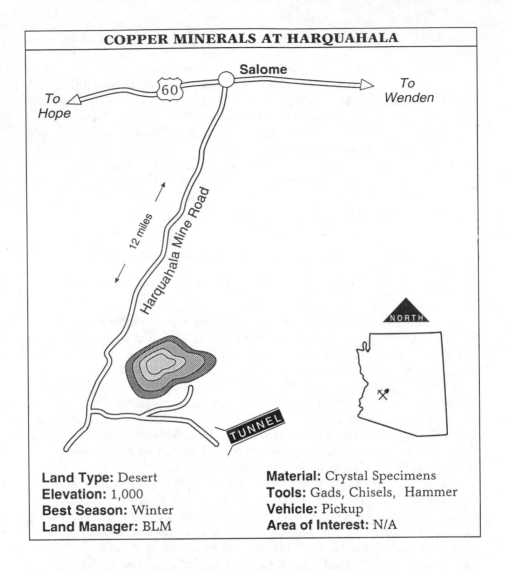

COPPER MINERALS AT HARQUAHALA

Salome

To Hope

60

To Wenden

12 miles

Harquahala Mine Road

NORTH

TUNNEL

Land Type: Desert
Elevation: 1,000
Best Season: Winter
Land Manager: BLM

Material: Crystal Specimens
Tools: Gads, Chisels, Hammer
Vehicle: Pickup
Area of Interest: N/A

SITE 66: *AGATE & ONYX NORTH OF WENDEN*

A variety of gemstone rough can be found within the foothills of the Buckskin Mountains, about twenty-five miles north of Wenden. The best of the material is a solid agate enclosing the manganese hieroglyphics called dendrites. An attractive red and green onyx is also available. Some collectors have reported finding a palm bog close by.

To reach the area, take the Alamo Lake Road north from Wenden, crossing through the Harcuvar Mountain Range at Cunningham Pass. Twelve miles north of Wenden, the road splits. Take the right-hand road for about one-half mile and the road will fork again, the right-hand fork going to Alamo Lake and the left-hand fork heading pretty much due north to the Buckskins. (You will be on the pipeline road.) Travel thirteen miles. Watch for a dim, two-track road leading to the right (east). Follow this primitive road for a little less than a mile and drive about one-half mile to the abandoned manganese mine.

The mine is a part of the Kaiserdoom Claims, located on May 2, 1918. The ore is in the form of pure psilomelane. Some of the nodules carry pockets of finely fibrous prismatic crystals within, probably manganite. The workings are deteriorated and dangerous.

The travertine onyx seems to be concentrated within a gully to the north

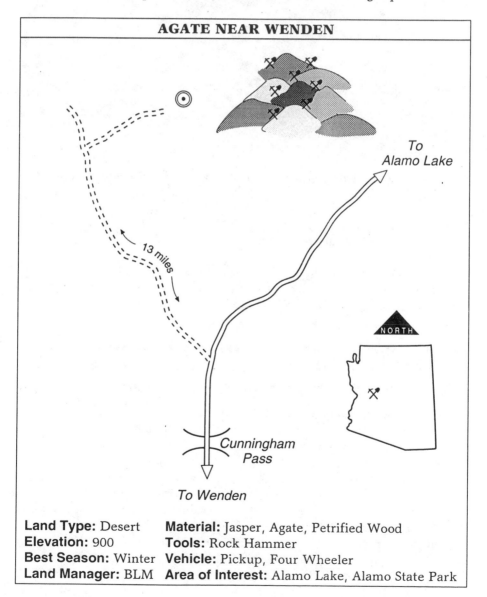

AGATE NEAR WENDEN

To Alamo Lake

13 miles

NORTH

Cunningham Pass

To Wenden

Land Type: Desert
Elevation: 900
Best Season: Winter
Land Manager: BLM

Material: Jasper, Agate, Petrified Wood
Tools: Rock Hammer
Vehicle: Pickup, Four Wheeler
Area of Interest: Alamo Lake, Alamo State Park

The author found a single piece of snow-white agate containing dendrites at Wenden site.

of the mine. Both the agate and the palm bog are on higher ground, among the dirty white hills southeast of the mine. Some collectors have reported discovering opalized palm here.

This collecting site is located far from the population centers and should not be attempted casually. A breakdown could cause a long stay. Summer temperatures are hot to the tenth power.

Alamo Lake State Park to the east would be a pleasant place to make camp. A number of other interesting collecting areas are nearby. If you tire of rock hunting (not likely), fishing and swimming are available.

SITE 67: *PATRIOTIC AGATE NEAR BRENDA*

Agate of outstanding quality can be found a few miles north of Brenda. Cobbles of a beautiful blue agate, somewhat similar to gem quality chrysocolla, have been collected from the low ridges north of the Bear Hills range. Other agate here shows a fiery red exterior (possibly jasper) and a snow white agate center, which sometimes is decorated with blood-red plumes.

The agate's exterior is coated with an orange rind that closely duplicates the crust on the cobbles of rhyolite that litter the ground. Separating the beauties from the beasts can take a sharp eye and a delicate stroke of the chipping hammer. Even if it goes against rockhound nature, it is often necessary to chip the cobbles to expose interior aspect. Done correctly, the moderate blow with the hammer will cause an insignificant conchoidal fracture at the small end of the cobble. The blow will window the material without creating internal fracturing.

To reach the collecting area, travel about three miles east of the junction with Interstate 10 on U.S. 60. Watch for a gated road to the left (north). Follow this primitive road for about 2.5 miles, watching for a road to the left (northwest). If you reach the lead mines, you have gone too far. Turn left and travel for four or five miles to an inconspicuous ridge. The agate is scattered over a one-half mile square area and may be present along other ridges in the area.

Those who enjoy prowling mine dumps will find the dumps of the lead

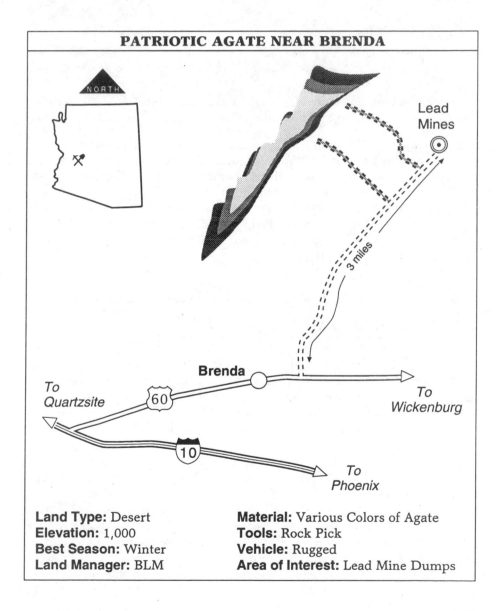

PATRIOTIC AGATE NEAR BRENDA

NORTH

Lead Mines

3 miles

Brenda

To Quartzsite

60

To Wickenburg

10

To Phoenix

Land Type: Desert
Elevation: 1,000
Best Season: Winter
Land Manager: BLM

Material: Various Colors of Agate
Tools: Rock Pick
Vehicle: Rugged
Area of Interest: Lead Mine Dumps

The Brenda agate beds contain material of unusual beauty.

mines interesting. The road leading to the mines and to the agate collecting area is a typical desert two-track. That means it starts out rough and deteriorates rapidly. Collectors who do not drive four-wheel-drive vehicles are advised to cross this trip from their list.

A number of houses have been constructed within this area in recent years, and the proliferation of roads might make it difficult to find the road that leads to the agate. Keep trying. Make local inquiry. The rock at the end of the road is well worth the effort.

SITE 68: *JASPER NEAR BRENDA*

The Bear Hills are a low range of volcanic hills that runs north and south of Brenda. The more impressive Plomosa Mountains can be seen to the west and the Ranegrass Plain is to the east. Within the south half of the Bear Hills is a deposit of attractive multicolored jasper. The best of the material shows red and yellow flowerlike patterns. Color ranges through the yellows, reds, oranges, and purples.

The area is easily accessible with about any type of vehicle. That accessibility, coupled with the nearness to the Quartzsite wintering grounds, causes the area to be heavily hit. Even so, quality material remains.

To reach the area, travel east on U.S. 60 through Brenda from its junction with Interstate 10. When you have driven for about five miles, you will notice a parking pullout to your right. The jasper is scattered on the slopes and on the flats that surround the southern half of these Bear Hills.

Much of the material is natural and rockhound-induced chippings. Do not ignore these chippings. Many are colorful and can be free-formed to produce attractive cabochons. Other material is chunky, up to grapefruit size. You likely will need a stout plastic or canvas carrying bucket to bring back the booty.

An obvious trail leads from the parking pullout, up over a low ridge, to end above an abandoned prospect. Search here for quality material.

Some of the Brenda jasper will pit during polishing. Use screen coated with silicon carbide (available at most hardware stores) to smooth away the pits and repolish, using a light touch to achieve a pit-free surface.

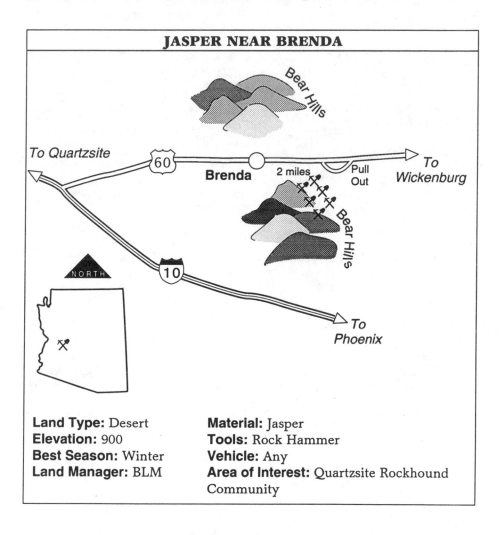

JASPER NEAR BRENDA

Land Type: Desert
Elevation: 900
Best Season: Winter
Land Manager: BLM

Material: Jasper
Tools: Rock Hammer
Vehicle: Any
Area of Interest: Quartzsite Rockhound Community

SITE 69: *MARBLE SOUTH OF SOCORRO PEAK*

A multicolored marble litters the slopes of a series of low hills that decorate the south slope of Socorro (Spanish for succor, or help) Peak. This is at the southwest end of the Harquahala Range. The material here is mostly pink. Some pieces include bands of orange and yellow. Part of the material holds interior cavities filled with a druse of crystals, most often quartz. Such cavities, when incorporated into the work, add eye appeal. As with most marble, the material here is best suited to serve as rough for bookends,

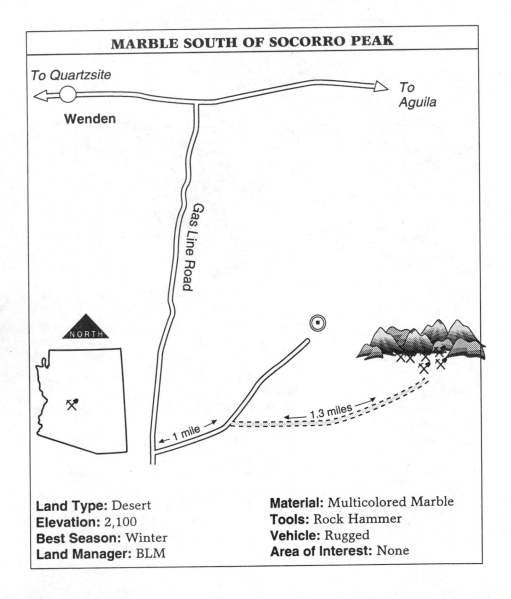

MARBLE SOUTH OF SOCORRO PEAK

To Quartzsite

Wenden

To Aguila

Gas Line Road

NORTH

1.3 miles

1 mile

Land Type: Desert
Elevation: 2,100
Best Season: Winter
Land Manager: BLM

Material: Multicolored Marble
Tools: Rock Hammer
Vehicle: Rugged
Area of Interest: None

spheres, carvings, and maybe even marbles (snicker). The best of the material can be worked into attractive cabochons.

The Socorro Peak marble is float from seams that "make" up on the mountain (at 5,681 feet, the highest peak within the Harquahala Range). The peak takes its name from the Socorro Mine, located in the 1880s by a group of prospectors from Socorro, New Mexico. A number of other mines and prospects pock the area.

A tough truck or other sort of rugged transportation is needed to make the drive to the best part of the collecting area. Those who have less rugged vehicles will be able to drive to within about a mile or so. The walk in is not all that bad if made during the mild winter season. The walk out with a load of marble is another matter entirely.

A cracking hammer and chisels can be assets here. Much of the marble is in hernia-sized chunks (you try to lift one, you get a hernia). Much of the marble is badly weathered on the surface. The cracking hammer and a chisel, or a gad, can be used to expose a fresh surface and can be used to reduce a keeper to pack-out size. Gloves and eye protectors are recommended.

SITE 70: *PLOMOSA MOUNTAIN AGATE*

A most attractive agate has been found on the east-facing slopes of the Plomosa (from the Spanish word for lead, as there are many lead mines in the area) Mountains. Agates and jaspers are present in generous number. Do not be in a hurry to fill the sack. Be selective. If your legs (and your lungs) are up to it, hike away from the road to prospect new country. Martin Koning, who some call the dean of Arizona rockhounds, labels this an under-explored and under-utilized gemstone field.

To reach the deposit, take Perry Lane (named for Raymond Perry, a man who has discovered many of the gemstone deposits of the area) north from the west edge of Brenda. About a mile in, you will come to a bifurcation. Take the left road for a bit more than two miles to the foothills of the Plomosa Mountains. Both sides of the road seem equally generous with the gemstone.

The Quartzsite Gem & Mineral Club has filed claim to part of the agate and jasper deposit. It will be necessary to join that club before you legally can collect the claims. A vast area remains unclaimed, however, and is legally accessible.

Summer temperatures here can reach the 120-degree mark, too hot for collecting and too hot for comfort. Winter temperatures are often shirt-sleeve comfortable. It is suggested that collecting trips be limited to between November 1 and the latter part of March.

The agate and jasper from the Plomosa Mountain field can be multicolored. Shades of red and orange dominate. Some specimens exhibit a medium green. The best material cuts and polishes to deliver outstanding cabochons.

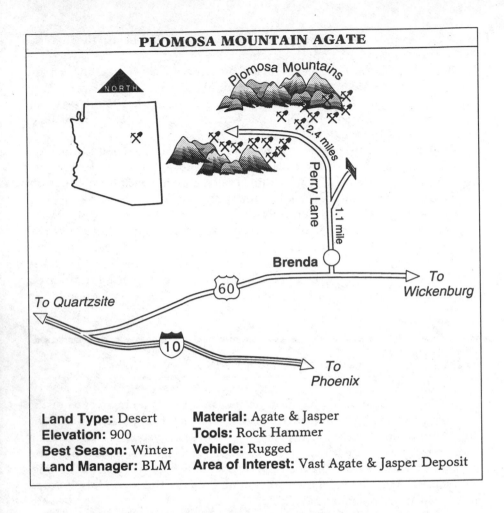

PLOMOSA MOUNTAIN AGATE

Plomosa Mountains

2.4 miles

Perry Lane

1.1 mile

Brenda

60

To Quartzsite

10

To Wickenburg

To Phoenix

Land Type: Desert
Elevation: 900
Best Season: Winter
Land Manager: BLM

Material: Agate & Jasper
Tools: Rock Hammer
Vehicle: Rugged
Area of Interest: Vast Agate & Jasper Deposit

SITE 71: *HEMATITE SOUTH OF BOUSE*

A series of shallow prospects has uncovered interesting hematite specimens within an area about three miles south and three miles west of Bouse.
The hematite is most commonly found in the typical botryoidal form. Some
prospects have exposed hematite that is roughly crystalline. Both kinds can
be found as float. Neither type is of cutting quality. Each is best used as
specimen material only. An attractive jasper is somewhat plentiful within the
same area. Color will range from red to yellow. Much of the jasper is weather-
worn, causing an unremarkable crust. Judicious chipping to expose a fresh
surface is usually a good technique.

A deposit of agate is located within the western edge of the Bouse Hills,
a bit south of the Barber Gene Mine. The agate is multicolored, fine grained,
and solid enough to take an excellent polish.

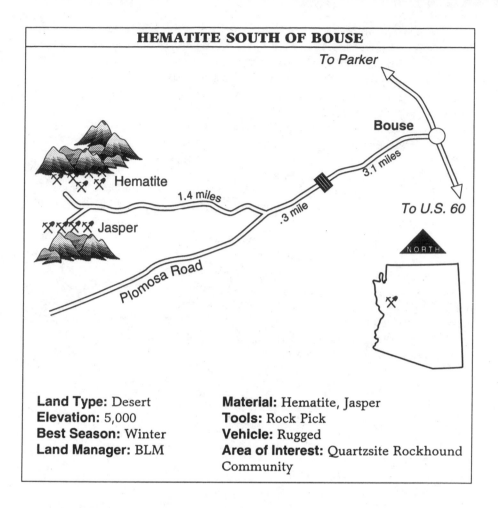

HEMATITE SOUTH OF BOUSE

To Parker

Bouse

3.1 miles

To U.S. 60

Hematite

1.4 miles

.3 mile

Jasper

Plomosa Road

NORTH

Land Type: Desert
Elevation: 5,000
Best Season: Winter
Land Manager: BLM

Material: Hematite, Jasper
Tools: Rock Pick
Vehicle: Rugged
Area of Interest: Quartzsite Rockhound Community

The word "bouse" is a mining term denoting ore mixed with veinstone, a second class ore that must be separated before the trip to the smelter. The town of Bouse (originally called Brayton), most likely, honors Thomas or George Bouse (maybe both), who were early residents.

SITE 72: *QUARTZ CRYSTALS AT QUARTZSITE*

Crystal Hill is located about nine miles south of Quartzsite; fifteen miles by road. The Bureau of Land Management has constructed an improved campground including cleared campsites and restrooms for the use of crystal collectors. There is no water here, however, so take an adequate supply.

The Crystal Hill quartz deposits have been hard hit. Thousands of rockhounds, many a part of the wintering contingent, collect here for many months of the year. Even so, crystals continue to be collected.

The casual collector will not leave with a bag of booty. Those who stroll the wash hoping to spot a maverick crystal will find the pickings slim. Collectors who philosophically oppose pick and shovel work, but who do not object to sifting through the debris left by other laborers, will be able to find a few crystals in the waste piles. Walkers and sifters who visit the deposit early in the fall, after summer inactivity at the site, might find a few crystals that have been exposed by the infrequent summer rains.

Diggers fare best at Crystal Hill, hard-rock miners who are able and willing to work the tough quartz seams that traverse the hill. Those fortunate enough to expose a crystal pocket are amply rewarded. The crystals pack the vugs, some in singles (a few are sceptered) and some in clusters. A good many show greenish chlorite inclusions.

Diggers should look to the hill north of the campground, where the quartz seams will be visible, as will the dozens of prospects excavated by previous collectors. Take your digging tools (pick, shovel, pry bar, chisels, gads, and hammers) and your heavy gloves, make the climb, and go to work. Do not neglect to take along material to protect the specimens during the walk out. Newspaper does a good job on these durable crystals. After being wrapped, they can be transported in about any kind of container or in a backpack.

The dry wash west of the campground can be a good place for the strollers.

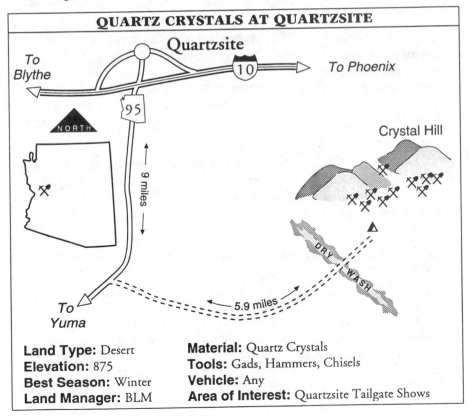

QUARTZ CRYSTALS AT QUARTZSITE

Quartzsite

To Blythe

To Phoenix

95

NORTH

Crystal Hill

9 miles

DRY WASH

To Yuma

5.9 miles

Land Type: Desert
Elevation: 875
Best Season: Winter
Land Manager: BLM

Material: Quartz Crystals
Tools: Gads, Hammers, Chisels
Vehicle: Any
Area of Interest: Quartzsite Tailgate Shows

Above: *Diggers in search of quality quartz follow a promising seam.* **Below:** *This hematite/quartz cooperation was found near Quartzsite.*

Those who make an early morning hunt (as soon as the sun comes up) will find the elusive quartz less difficult to see. With the sun behind you, the clear quartz will sometimes throw back a termination reflection.

Limit your collecting here to the winter months. Summer temperatures can, and often do, exceed 120 degrees Fahrenheit. Even some winter days can be uncomfortably warm. Many collectors work the cooler morning hours and then shade up during the heat of the day. The hill does not cool appreciably until sundown.

To reach the area, drive south from Quartzsite on Arizona 95 for nine miles. Turn left on the Crystal Hill Road and drive the six miles to the campground. The road, although dirt, is maintained. Nearly any kind of vehicle can make it to the campground.

SITE 73: *CRYSTALS SOUTHWEST OF QUARTZSITE*

The low hills that surround the town of Quartzsite are pocked with prospect holes. Some of these are shallow diggings and others have been developed to a surprising depth. The dumps of some of these diggings, or an exposed vein within the prospect, may yield up interesting crystals.

The best is the quartz and ilmenite crystallizations found in a series of mine dumps about six miles west-southwest of Quartzsite. A good specimen of the quartz-ilmenite can be spectacular.

The road to the diggings is rough. Collectors who do not own a high-clearance vehicle should bypass this one.

The mines here are intermittently active. **If the property is posted,**

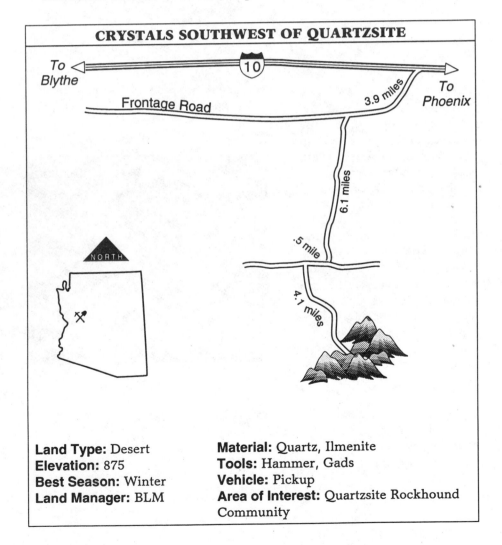

CRYSTALS SOUTHWEST OF QUARTZSITE

To Blythe

10

To Phoenix

Frontage Road

3.9 miles

6.1 miles

.5 mile

NORTH

4.1 miles

Land Type: Desert
Elevation: 875
Best Season: Winter
Land Manager: BLM

Material: Quartz, Ilmenite
Tools: Hammer, Gads
Vehicle: Pickup
Area of Interest: Quartzsite Rockhound Community

respect the private property rights. Walking the slopes below the dumps will sometimes produce specimens of interest.

A deposit of travertine onyx is located nearby. Brown-on-brown patterns within the onyx add interest. This material will polish about like the onyx from other Arizona deposits; that is, poorly. The high calcite content causes the material to accept the polish reluctantly.

A low-grade chert is also present. The color is mostly pale and uninteresting.

SITE 74: *AGATE & CHALCEDONY NEAR PALM CANYON*

Palm Canyon is one of the few places in Arizona where native palms (Washingtonia arizonica) can be found. A decent trail leads to the palm tree site. Good quality agate and chalcedony have been found near the road that leads east from State Road 95 to the trailhead. The deposit is within the KOFA Wildlife Refuge. **Collecting is limited to surface material: No digging is permitted.**

This orbicular jasper was found south of Stone Cabin.

About six miles south of the Palm Canyon turnoff on State Road 95, a dirt road leads to a cluster of low hills located to the left (east) of State Road 95. Those hills hold a tan to brown pastelite. You will notice a cluster of "gopher holes" left by previous collectors. Dig close by or wander to look for float.

Another collecting site is located a bit more than five miles farther south on State Road 95. A deep wash that borders the east side of the highway holds an interesting orbicular rhyolite. The base color is brown (as one would expect of rhyolite) and the interior is patterned with well defined "eyes" of

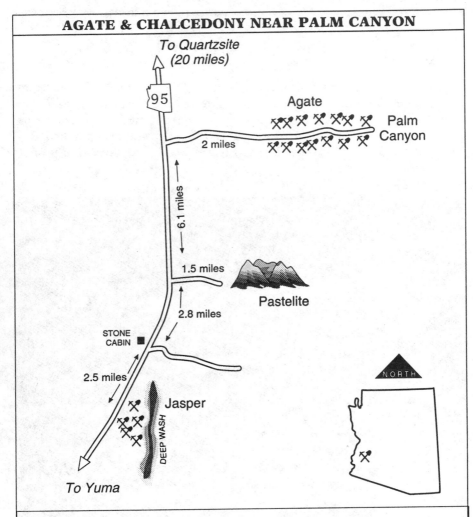

AGATE & CHALCEDONY NEAR PALM CANYON

To Quartzsite (20 miles)

95

Agate

Palm Canyon

2 miles

6.1 miles

1.5 miles

Pastelite

2.8 miles

STONE CABIN

NORTH

2.5 miles

Jasper

DEEP WASH

To Yuma

Land Type: Desert
Elevation: 800
Best Season: Winter
Land Manager: BLM

Material: Orbicular Rhyolite
Tools: Pick, Shovel, Hammer
Vehicle: Any
Area of Interest: Quartzsite Rockhound Community

a lighter brown. The material makes fine rough for bookends, spheres, and carvings. Some of the best of the material can be cut and polished to obtain decent cabochons.

The orbicular rhyolite grades to jasper in some specimens. The deposit is located near the northwest end of the Castle Dome Range, a range that is home to a healthy herd of desert bighorn sheep. The highest peak in the range, at 3,821 feet, was named Capitol Dome by early-day miners. That name was eventually corrupted to the present Castle Dome.

The Castle Dome Mine, located near the west edge of the range, has given up interesting crystals of cerussite. The most successful collectors use a screen to sift through a very fine part of the dump. The author, collecting underground here in about 1967, narrowly escaped death as a twelve-by-twelve shaft shoring gave way. The mine is in worse shape today and is therefore even more dangerous. The best mineral specimen in the world, or a box full, could not entice the author there again. Cerussite and vanadinite (yellow) were recovered.

The Castle Dome ore was hauled by burro back to the Colorado River at Castle Dome Landing (originally called Pitoti), taken by Steamboat to Yuma, and then shipped to San Francisco for smelting.

Specimens of fluorite have also been recovered from the mine dumps; not surprising, since some of the ore consisted of a roughly crystalline fluorite.

SITE 75: *FIRE AGATE AT KOFA*

The KOFA mountain range is a rugged mix of hills and canyons that roughly parallels Arizona's western boundary. The area is highly mineralized and contains many mines and prospects. The name KOFA comes from one such mine, the King of Arizona, called K of A by early miners. The entire KOFA range is within the desert bighorn sheep protectorate established by the U.S. Fish & Wildlife Service. Much of the wildlife refuge has been declared a roadless area. Only the most important roads within the area remain open to vehicle travel. The road that leads to the fire agate deposit remains open as of publication, but the status can change.

The KOFA Wildlife Refuge is not a wildlife sanctuary. Desert bighorn sheep and desert mule deer are hunted during fall and winter. **Surface collecting of rocks and minerals is permitted. Digging for rocks and minerals, or for anything else, is prohibited.** The KOFA chalcedony "makes" in narrow cracks within the country rock (rhyolite). The chalcedony is attached to each wall of the crack. It is unusually attractive, consisting of large smooth bubbles, sometimes surrounded by poorly formed quartz crystals. Much of the material carries the sardonyx that carries the fire. The author has recovered pieces up to dinner-plate size.

The cracks that carry the chalcedony are dirt-filled, thus making the in situ chalcedony inaccessible. A limited amount of surface material is available as float, but the likelihood of finding decent material on the surface is remote.

The refuge provides an opportunity to see and photograph the rare desert bighorn sheep. Blinds constructed near waterholes can offer a closeup look at the sheep during summer. (It is hot, hot, hot.)

To obtain current information on the KOFA National Wildlife Refuge, write to Box 1032, Yuma, AZ 85364.

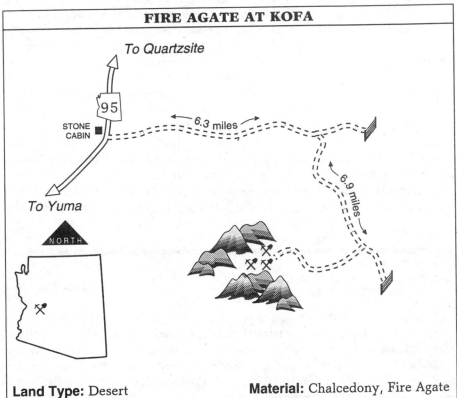

FIRE AGATE AT KOFA

Land Type: Desert
Elevation: 800
Best Season: Winter
Land Manager: Kofa Wildlife Refuge

Material: Chalcedony, Fire Agate
Tools: None, Surface Only
Vehicle: Rugged
Area of Interest: Desert Bighorn Sheep Refuge

GLOSSARY

Aggregate	A mixture of different rocks.
Basalt	A dark igneous rock formed from a lava flow, often shaped in columns.
Batholith	A large mass of igneous rock hardened beneath the Earth's surface, such as granite, often thrust upward to form mountains, as in the Bradhsaw Mountains.
Brachiopod	A marine animal similar to a mollusk, with both dorsal and ventral shells.
Cab	See cabochon.
Cabochon	A gemstone shaped into a dome or oval and polished.
Carat	A unit of weight for gemstones. One carat equals 200 milligrams.
Chalcedony	A microcrystalline variety of quartz.
Concretion	A transparent or translucent cryptocrystalline variety of quartz.
Dendritic	In the shape of a branched tree, as when minerals crystallize in minute fractures within rocks.
Facet	A small, flat plane cut onto the surface of a gem.
Fossil	The remains or impressions of plants and animals preserved in rock.
Gad	A pointed tool for breaking up rock.
Gangue	The rocky or earthy minerals occurring with the metallic ore in a vein or deposit.

Gouge	A layer of decomposed rocks or minerals along the wall of a vein.
Grizzly	A large mesh or grid of metal bars used to screen ore.
Igneous	Rock that hardened from molten material.
Inclusion	A lump of one mineral enclosed within another mineral.
Japanese Twinning	A rare pairing of crystal terminations, formed at a specific angle from one prism, with the appearance of Mickey Mouse ears.
Lapidary	An artist who cuts, polishes, and sometimes engraves gemstones.
Lode	A vein-like deposit of minerals contained within bedrock or other rock formation.
Metamorphic	Rock that has undergone a change in structure or chemical composition due to extreme heat or pressure within the Earth's crust.
Micromount	Mineral specimens mounted for viewing under a microscope.
Ore	Metal-bearing mineral or rock, especially in reference to a deposit that can be worked or mined.
Overburden	Waste dirt and rock covering a mineral deposit.
Peridot	A translucent variety of the mineral olivine.
Petrification	The process by which organic material is impregnated with silica or other minerals, preserving the cell structure in stone as the silica solidifies.

Petroglyph	A drawing or design chiseled or pecked into the face of a rock by prehistoric people.
Pictograph	A drawing or design painted onto a rock face by prehistoric people.
Porphyry	Any rock containing coarse crystals in a finer-grained mass.
Prism	The polygonal body of a crystal.
Pseudomorph	A crystal with the geometric appearance of one mineral that has been chemically replaced with another mineral.
Sedimentary	Rock formed by the deposition, compaction, and cementation of sediment.
Stopes	Excavations within a mine, typically at the end of shafts or tunnels, where the ore has been removed.
Sump	A pit in a mine where water collects, often the bottom of a shaft or in the floor of a passageway.
Terminations	The end or point of a crystal.
Thumbnail Specimen	A small piece of mineral, generally less than one cubic inch.
Twinning	A crystalline form; two crystals extending from a single prism. See Japanese Twinning
Vein	Any body or layer of mineral or metal clearly separated or defined from the surrounding rock.
Vug	A small cavity in a rock.

ABOUT THE AUTHOR

Gerry Blair has roamed the Arizona outback for more than half a century. He has spent much of that time rockhounding—pursuing the wily wulfenite and the elusive agate to the depths of dismal mines and to the rare air of high mountain peaks. On one rockhounding expedition, he stripped to his shorts (not a pretty sight) and dove into icy sumps to grope for crystallizations. He is, in short, a gem and mineral hound, one of the most experienced and knowledgeable rockhounds in Arizona. Blair ended a twenty-five-year law enforcement career in 1976 when he retired from his position as Northern Zone Commander for the Arizona Highway Patrol. Now a prolific author, he has written more than 500 magazine articles and is a contributing editor for *Rock and Gem Magazine*. *Rockhounding Arizona* is his sixth book. Gerry Blair shows an interest in every field of the rock, gem, and mineral hobby. He owns a particularly fine collection of Arizona minerals, many self-collected. He is an award-winning lapidary and a talented silversmith. He has served as a gem, mineral, and jewelry judge for many competitions. Blair and his wife Ann live among the ponderosa pines in Flagstaff, Arizona, with Grandma, a German short-haired pointer, and Inky, a particularly homely Sharpei.

INDEX

INDEX

INDEX

FALCON GUIDES® Leading the Way™

■ *To order any of these books, check with your local bookseller
or call FALCON® at* **1-800-582-2665**.
Visit us on the world wide web at:
www.FalconOutdoors.com

FALCON®

FALCON GUIDES® Leading the way™

FalconGuides® are available for where-to-go hiking, mountain biking, rock climbing, walking, scenic driving, fishing, rockhounding, paddling, birding, wildlife viewing, and camping. We also have FalconGuides on essential outdoor skills and subjects and field identification. The following titles are currently available, but this list grows every year. For a free catalog with a complete list of titles, call FALCON toll-free at 1-800-582-2665.

Birding Guides
Birding Minnesota
Birding Montana
Birding Northern California
Birding Texas
Birding Utah

Rockhounding Guides
Rockhounding Arizona
Rockhounding California
Rockhounding Colorado
Rockhounding Montana
Rockhounding Nevada
Rockhound's Guide to
   New Mexico
Rockhounding Texas
Rockhounding Utah
Rockhounding Wyoming

Walking
Walking Colorado Springs
Walking Denver
Walking Portland
Walking St. Louis
Walking Virginia Beach

Camping Guides
Camping California's
   National Forests
Camping Colorado
Camping Southern California
Camping Washington

All Field Guides
Bitterroot: Montana State Flower
Canyon Country Wildflowers
Central Rocky Mountain
   Wildflowers
Great Lakes Berry Book
New England Berry Book
Ozark Wildflowers
Pacific Northwest Berry Book
Plants of Arizona
Rare Plants of Colorado
Rocky Mountain Berry Book
Scats & Tracks of the Pacific
   Coast States
Scats & Tracks of the Rocky Mtns.
Southern Rocky Mountain
   Wildflowers
Tallgrass Prairie Wildflowers
Western Trees
Wildflowers of Southwestern Utah
Willow Bark and Rosehips

Paddling Guides
Floater's Guide to Colorado
Paddling Minnesota
Paddling Montana
Paddling Okefenokee
Paddling Oregon
Paddling Yellowstone & Grand
   Teton National Parks

How-to Guides
Avalanche Aware
Backpacking Tips
Bear Aware
Desert Hiking Tips
Hiking with Dogs
Leave No Trace
Mountain Lion Alert
Reading Weather
Route Finding
Using GPS
Wilderness First Aid
Wilderness Survival

More Guidebooks
Backcountry Horseman's
   Guide to Washington
Camping California's
   National Forests
Exploring Canyonlands & Arches
   National Parks
Exploring Hawaii's Parklands
Exploring Mount Helena
Recreation Guide to WA
   National Forests
Touring California & Nevada
   Hot Springs
Trail Riding Western
   Montana
Wild Country Companion
Wilderness Directory
Wild Montana
Wild Utah

■ *To order any of these books, check with your local bookseller*
*or call FALCON ® at **1-800-582-2665**.*
Visit us on the world wide web at:
www.FalconOutdoors.com

FALCON®

FALCON GUIDES ® Leading the Way™

WILDLIFE VIEWING GUIDES

Alaska Wildlife Viewing Guide
Arizona Wildlife Viewing Guide
California Wildlife Viewing Guide
Colorado Wildlife Viewing Guide
Florida Wildlife Viewing Guide
Indiana Wildlife Viewing Guide
Iowa Wildlife Viewing Guide
Kentucky Wildlife Viewing Guide
Massachusetts Wildlife Viewing Guide
Montana Wildlife Viewing Guide
Nebraska Wildlife Viewing Guide
Nevada Wildlife Viewing Guide
New Hampshire Wildlife Viewing Guide
New Jersey Wildlife Viewing Guide
New Mexico Wildlife Viewing Guide
New York Wildlife Viewing Guide
North Carolina Wildlife Viewing Guide
North Dakota Wildlife Viewing Guide
Ohio Wildlife Viewing Guide
Oregon Wildlife Viewing Guide
Puerto Rico and the Virgin Islands WVG
Tennessee Wildlife Viewing Guide
Texas Wildlife Viewing Guide
Utah Wildlife Viewing Guide
Vermont Wildlife Viewing Guide
Virginia Wildlife Viewing Guide
Washington Wildlife Viewing Guide
West Virginia Wildlife Viewing Guide
Wisconsin Wildlife Viewing Guide

HISTORIC TRAIL GUIDES

Traveling California's Gold Rush Country
Traveling the Lewis & Clark Trail
Traveling the Oregon Trail
Traveler's Guide to the Pony Express Trail

SCENIC DRIVING GUIDES

Scenic Driving Alaska and the Yukon
Scenic Driving Arizona
Scenic Driving the Beartooth Highway
Scenic Driving California
Scenic Driving Colorado
Scenic Driving Florida
Scenic Driving Georgia
Scenic Driving Hawaii
Scenic Driving Idaho
Scenic Driving Michigan
Scenic Driving Minnesota
Scenic Driving Montana
Scenic Driving New England
Scenic Driving New Mexico
Scenic Driving North Carolina
Scenic Driving Oregon
Scenic Driving the Ozarks including the
   Ouchita Mountains
Scenic Driving Pennsylvania
Scenic Driving Texas
Scenic Driving Utah
Scenic Driving Washington
Scenic Driving Wisconsin
Scenic Driving Wyoming
Scenic Driving Yellowstone & Grand Teton
   National Parks
Back Country Byways
Scenic Byways East
Scenic Byways Farwest
Scenic Byways Rocky Mountains

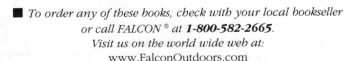

■ *To order any of these books, check with your local bookseller*
*or call FALCON ® at **1-800-582-2665**.*
Visit us on the world wide web at:
www.FalconOutdoors.com